PARENTS, LISTEN UP

PARENTS, LISTEN UP

leading teenagers to grit, resilience
and a love of learning

Marilyn Englander

The stories in this book do not identify any particular individuals. They are based on true events that occurred over the course of almost three decades in many different classrooms, in several different schools. No individuals are intended to be identified. All names and identifications have been omitted and circumstances as well as locations have been changed to protect privacy. Names used in the stories are purely fictional, and not the real names of individuals. The genders, circumstances, personal traits and other details of individuals have been changed, and in some cases, fictionalized, or composite stories have been created to express general themes. The essential storylines repeated over and over again, one school to another, year after year, exposing some universal truths about how school is for adolescents.

ISBN: 1974006557
ISBN 13: 9781974006557
Library of Congress Control Number: 2017911889
CreateSpace Independent Publishing Platform
North Charleston, South Carolina

Table of Contents

Preface

Your kid's middle school or high school teacher is actually a front line spy. Or maybe a teen whisperer. But certainly a parent's strongest ally. Or could be.

I have lived with teenagers, watched them and listened to them, for more than 25 years. Teaching has been enormously fulfilling and all consuming. I thrived on working with the kids. Yet as I witnessed changes in the quality of their lives over those years, I saw a lot that was not pretty. It troubled me. Education was derailing.

I believed there was a better way to educate teenagers, and I felt frustrated by many of the practices I'd observed in the various schools where I'd taught. My concern motivated me to found a small independent middle school. In 2005, my teaching partner and I opened REAL School Marin. The school enjoyed eleven vigorous years of pioneering a new model for educating twelve- to fifteen-year-olds. I was excited about the success our students found, and realized we had made important discoveries about effective and meaningful school reform.

In this book, I take the reader behind the scenes in private education and reveal what is really going on, for both students and teachers. I speak from my own experience as an educator as well as for the many colleagues I interviewed, those who have taught middle school, high school, and college.

In addition, I have benefited from another perspective: I am a parent of two children, now grown up. I know the scene when kids come home from school each day.

Both teachers and parents invest enormous energy and passion in overseeing the education of children. One would think these adults would see the process similarly, but that could not be further from the truth. To put it in the simplest terms, a gaping divide exists between parents struggling to get what they *feel* is the best for their kids and teachers struggling to deliver what they *know from experience* is best for students.

As parents, we feel we know our own kids best, and we're convinced we're superior judges of what they need from school. Teachers, on the other hand, have the advantage of having seen what works and what does not, for hundreds of students, over and over again through many years. They are professionally trained to draw out students' greatest potential. Often, this entails setting up big challenges and coaching children over enormous hurdles. It can be a painful process that is difficult to watch and hard to sustain, but the struggle is the very essence of personal growth, intellectual and otherwise. A parent's role is to nurture, love, protect, and defend the child: parents are trained, so to speak, to be fast-twitch responders. Otherwise, a lot of toddlers would hit the sidewalk or fall off the climbing structure every day. It is antithetical to the role of parents to condone pain or frustration.

In an ideal situation, parents and teachers work together to find a balance—to push kids just hard enough so that they will surmount obstacles without feeling utter defeat. Cooperation of this sort works fairly well through the elementary school years, and the tension between parents and teachers is usually minimal. But come the onset of puberty, there is a sea change. Adolescents must and do push away from parents while at the same time experiencing a period of explosive intellectual growth. Their brains are developing as fast as they did during the toddler stage. Such vigorous growth demands guidance, fertilization, and pruning. This is where teachers can make the critical difference, getting in there where most parents are no longer effective, or welcome.

REAL School Marin was founded on a model that provides adolescents with powerful stimuli and a framework for robust, successful learning. Our theory reaps big rewards, but many of our practices strike parents as too hard, too demanding, and they fear their kids are too fragile to handle the stress. Nevertheless, we have seen our students thrive on being pushed, goaded, and propelled by their own willpower to surmount daunting obstacles.

The very experiences that students need the most are too often those that parents want to avoid. Seeking to maintain calm and peace on the home front, they want to cherry-pick a school or opt for "storefront" one-on-one alternative educational settings in which their kids "will be happy." The current national debate about educational reform capitalizes on parents' weariness and upset at the inevitably messy process of learning and growing that all children must undertake. Who would not be lured by the promise of a sunny-faced child coming home from school every day, having had a lot of fun? The voucher system appears to offer parents a means to control their children's maturation experience: to pay for private education that will make their kids happy and avoid upsets.

However, my students themselves come back to report to me that the rigorous demands and big challenges we gave them set them up for success. The tasks we assigned that made them step outside their comfort zones gave them the grit they needed to be strong enough to make it through the years that followed. They say that what we asked of them changed them forever, for the better.

Whether your teenager is slamming doors and shouting, sitting slumped over a phone for hours, or treating you to sullen silence in the car, there's a very different kid interacting with the teacher at school all day. Most often for the parent, it's that kid he wishes he could see more of.

The teacher, though routinely maligned for assigning all that homework and being stingy with the As, can stand in for parents when a kid reaches adolescence and begins, in a very healthy way, to push away. A seasoned teacher has seen it all, fortunately. Hundreds of kids pass through her hands over the years, and that means a lot of perspective gained.

In these pages, I explain what we learned in designing a better middle school, how we did it, where the traps and the false leads are. We can do a much better job educating our teenagers; they are tougher and more capable than adults could ever imagine.

The chapters of this book alternate between narrative descriptions of what goes on at school—with a liberal helping of irreverent humor—and analytical discussions of the world that adolescents inhabit and of how mainstream attempts to educate them are going awry. I offer examples of practices that work to get students back on course.

The stories I tell are based on true events that occurred over the course of almost three decades in many different classrooms, in several different schools. All names, personal traits, locations and circumstances have been changed to protect privacy. But the essential storylines repeated over and over again, student after student, one school to another, year after year. I believe the stories expose some universal truths about how school is for kids.

A majority of the problems in private schools today are the products of the impact of money and influence. Too often, when parents purchase a pricey commodity (private school tuition), they feel entitled to demand custom options, to bargain for a "better fit," to object to any or all practices or standards, to reject features they don't like, or to insist that the community eject undesirable members. Trying to satisfy the customer is no way to design an educational program, yet that is exactly what happens when money drives what happens at school. Private schools wage an incessant struggle trying to work with parents who believe they know more about education than the educators do, or want a better deal for their own student.

I am indebted to my teaching colleagues who talked endlessly with me about their own experiences. They complained, exalted, endured, and road tested the new practices that we were developing in our school. I am grateful to those parents who saw the fruits of our new model and gave me their trust without criticizing or micromanaging.

Family, friends, and colleagues read and commented on the project as a whole and on different versions of the manuscript, over many years' time. Special thanks to Clair Englander, Megan Englander, Doug Kerr, Sue Campbell, Karin Kramer Baldwin, David Baldwin, Christine Price, and Mark Trautwein. Their input made all the difference.

Early versions of the material in chapters 9 and 14 were published in *Independent School Magazine*, the winter 2016 edition, in the chapter "Our New Priority: Community-Building Skills at the Center." Short versions of several chapters were aired on the program *Perspectives* on KQED radio, San Francisco.

I owe unending thanks to my stalwart teaching partner, Mark Biglieri. He courageously agreed to open a new school with me, a crazy adventure. Together, we started a little revolution in adolescent education. Margot Koch made enormous contributions by joining our team part time as well.

Finally, infinite gratitude and thanks to my husband, Curt, and children Ben and Jean. They lived in the eye of the storm all these years but never stopped cheering me on.

November 2017

Introduction

INTO THEIR HANDS WE DELIVER THE FUTURE OF AMERICA

Schoolteachers are not like window washers, but they get treated the same way. The parents have no idea of the things I see or what their kids tell me. Because, unlike the window washer — whose view can be cut off if you close the blinds— the teacher has an unobstructed 24/7 view of every family's life. Teachers spend hours and hours each day with other people's children, far more time than parents themselves do.

I know she knows her parents are thinking of a divorce before they know she knows. The daughter told me one day after school when we were stacking books.

Her dad hits her when she doesn't understand the math homework.

His mom suggested he just watch the movie online, so he didn't have to bother to read the novel assigned for English class.

He is gay, and we know he is terrified his family will find out, but at school we all just go with it, no big deal, since we've known forever.

There are scary money troubles at home.

His parents are writing the high school application essays because they don't trust him to do a good enough job.

And on and on.

Kids say the darnedest things, as Art Linkletter told us in the 1950s. They still do. And who's listening? Your kid's teacher is.

The thing is this: kids have a tough time with discretion. So it all comes tumbling out at school. We hear about the shortcuts the adults use to get ahead. One teenager brags that his dad said that what counts is money, not learning American history. And they report unsavory comments from home about women, immigrants, people of other races.

Like it or not, your kid's teacher knows everything about your home life.

Teaching school is a goldmine for an amateur sociologist—an enlightening, often sad, frequently poignant view into how families live today. But few people understand what goes on at school. In the classroom, we do so much of what used to get done at home. We feed kids lunch—even the wealthy ones, who are often hungry. We check their heads for lice. We teach them how to hold a fork (even in the seventh grade), answer a phone, address an envelope, use deodorant, tell time, read a calendar, sweep the floor, plunge a toilet, use a dictionary, read a map, find birth control. We talk about morality and God, even though they are not in the curriculum. We explain why it is not right to lie about your age to get into the movies for cheaper. We discuss the hard stuff like genocide, human trafficking, social injustice.

In this country, teaching is a low-status, discard profession:

> "Those who can, do. Those who can't, teach."
> "Schoolteachers only work a seven-hour day."

"June, July, and August: the three best reasons to teach."
"They just work with kids, for god's sake. What's so hard about sixth grade math? There's an app for that."

There is an alarming disconnect between how society looks at teachers and the work asked of them. Into their hands we deliver the entire future of America, every single person in the next generation— to be educated, guided, and influenced. Teachers are on the front line, molding the future.

And yet, the system often pits parents against teachers. In the race to the top—to the best jobs, to the most secure future—parents often view teachers with hostility. They stand in the way of Johnny's moving forward—all those grades and tests and homework. It is *us* versus *them*, my kid against the school in a struggle to get ahead.

Not all parents sense this friction, but teachers surely do. From my friend who teaches in an inner-city elementary school to colleagues teaching in suburban middle schools to another who polishes high school students to enter Dartmouth— all report daily upsets with parents who, at the very least, question and challenge them. More often, the parents suspect, criticize, and attack them.

To survive, teachers have to keep an arsenal of black humor in their hip pockets. We have nicknames—in self-defense—for the parents who make our lives the toughest: "Billion-Dollar Mom," "Is-It-OK-If-I'm-Late-to-Pick-Him-Up Dad," "I-Only-Did-a-Little-of-His-Homework Mom."

I began to realize that I have always enjoyed a special view behind the scenes, having been in classrooms since my twenties but also raising two kids of my own. I straddled the line between teacher and parent. But because of that, I did not get the secret communal memos that shaped what other moms and dads thought and did:

> "Start to cry in the parent-teacher conference, and the teacher will ease up on your kid."
> "Make sure the teacher knows your kid is super sensitive."
> "Email that teacher about every mistake she makes. Don't let her get away with anything."
> "Demand the teacher respond immediately to your complaints and not put you off."
> "Take it very seriously when your kid tells you how wicked that teacher is."

Teachers live in kids' hip pockets. We see them and listen to them when they know the parents aren't around, and forget we are. We've learned a lot that parents and school reformers as well really ought to know.

It could be that folks just don't know how it looks and feels on the other side of the divide that is the classroom door. As a teacher, I have witnessed the disconnect that this causes and the damage that it does. Schools fail when they give in to parents' demands for changes that they think will make school more comfortable, less stressful, more fun. Meanwhile, the kids cynically learn to game the system and defeat their own growth. I have watched many kids as they begin to believe that trying hard is just not worth the effort.

Maybe no one really has a clue about what goes on at school. Maybe the teacher that we have all feared our entire lives is actually a trustworthy guide who can help navigate the jungle of the teenage years. Parents pushing for school reform, access to vouchers, and school choice have a very limited view of what is happening behind the classroom door.

So I thought I would teach some special lessons on the scene at school, what it is like to teach, and offer some clues about where we are going wrong and how we can do a better job of educating the next generation.

So, parents, listen up. It's time for a little tell-all.

Practicing Psychiatry without a License

For many years, before I founded REAL School Marin, I taught in another middle school. My homeroom class had twenty-eight students. They came from affluent families who lived in "good" neighborhoods. The children of plenty and of privilege. But they were just like all the other kids.

I worked with these kids for 170 days each year. I was with them seven or more hours a day. Considering commute time, parents' work schedules, cooking dinner, housework, homework, and what have you, I spent about four times as much time with my students as their parents did. I was in the thick of it. All teachers are.

For starters, consider what I did on a typical morning, any old day, at school:

Unlock doors to school hallways at 7:30 a.m. Notice student sulkily leaning against the wall.
Comfort student who had a fight with her mom on the way to school.
See student arrive in tears. She has lost her new soccer shoes.

Help kid open his locker.

Start down hall to open bathrooms but first stop to help kid whose binder just exploded.

Unlock student bathrooms.

Begin to clean off white board, get interrupted.

Help kid with late homework. Hear about his dad yelling at him over it last night.

Unfreeze computer for kid trying to print out his essay.

Go make coffee in office. Find a memo announcing lunchtime staff meeting.

Have three impromptu parent conferences by the parent mailbox cubbies. Each one asks for "just a sec," but it takes fifteen minutes.

Copy handouts for the day. Fix photocopier when the paper jams.

Use pliers to open another locker.

Teach kid what to do for milk spilled inside his backpack.

Overhear two kids' conversation about the party Saturday night. Make note to check in with parents about the alcohol.

Shoo dog off campus.

Turn down a parent who wants "a quick conference," with one minute to go until the bell.

Take roll and figure out if excuses are legitimate for the three kids who are late.

Teach a small group for thirty minutes.

Switch groups and begin the lesson again with the second half of class. Teach thirty minutes.

Help girl crying in back of classroom over lord-knows-what that occurred last period.

Try to bring up a video clip on the computer. Screen freezes, so write info on the white board.

Teach forty-five minutes.

Give kids a problem to solve on paper while I remove one kid from class and take him outside for disciplinary chat.

Answer questions from a private tutor who interrupts class.

Return phone call to parent.

Make an ice pack for a girl who has smashed her finger between chair and desk.

Make phone call to therapist treating a student.

Call to schedule field trip for January.

Administer morning dose of Ritalin to a student.

Write a quick article on a class activity for school's weekly newsletter.

Provide impromptu parent conference to mom who arrives with a lost lunch.

Clean up courtyard: candy wrappers, plastic bags, soda cans, lost soccer shoes!

Haul out first-aid kit for student who tore off fingernail in physical education (PE) and also hear about dog that died.

Counsel a student kicked out of PE: fifteen minutes and lots of tissues.

Start yard duty at morning break, and it's still only 10:30 a.m.!

A teacher drills math facts, explains weather and geography, coaches legible handwriting, reveals the secret of writing a five-point essay. But he or she is also pressed into practicing psychiatry without a license, working as a triage nurse, imparting lessons on morality, standing in for distracted or overworked parents. Kids soak up the values and opinions that teachers offer while they figure out who they are in counterpoint to the person standing at the head of the classroom. It can be inspiring work, or a terrifying power trip.

Actress Maggie Smith said it best when playing a teacher in the film version of Muriel Spark's *The Prime of Miss Jean Brodie*: "Give me a girl at an impressionable age and she is mine for life." Teachers have a breadth and depth of influence on children that cannot be underestimated or ignored.

But they also have a view behind the curtain into the private lives of all their students. As teachers, we are charged to dispense knowledge and form minds, but we are also required to observe, to take note, to notice.

Routinely, the teacher is the first to notice black and blue marks on a kid that are the giveaway about abuse in the home. A casual conversation about that will unravel the whole situation, with schoolmates adding facts that no adult could get at. We are the ones who have to make the wrenching call to Child Protective Services. We are required to report.

Terrified of talking to her mother, a thirteen-year-old will let slip to a teacher that she is afraid she is pregnant. She admits that her parents think she goes jogging after school, but two blocks away she meets up with an older boy.

We see cut marks on a girl's wrists when, sitting in the sun on the picnic table at lunchtime, she peels off that ratty hoodie. She didn't forget: she wanted it to be noticed. Teachers are the ones who will be calling the parents.

The grandfather who volunteers to drive on a field trip casually gives the teacher an earful about the scene at home. We find out the mother berates her kid for being fat, and there is a much older drug-addicted sister. No wonder that when this boy runs away from home, he texts his teacher. Wanting to be found.

The burden teachers assume is one they have taken on willingly, with enormous idealism. Everyone needs what teachers offer. The emotional distance they can maintain, precisely because they are not the parents, and the broad experience they have had with hundreds of kids are valuable assets. It is worth it to understand and empathize with these folks who are raising America for all of us. The parents who portray teachers as too tough, too obstructionist, too meddling, too unsympathetic are firing at their very best front line troops.

There are a thousand stories to tell. Each one is true. Names and specifics are changed here, but the situations as they unfolded are authentic. Seared into my memory and etched behind my eyelids, and unfortunately, repeated year after year.

Behind the scenes at school, the truth comes out.

2

Pay to Play in Private School

Sending your kid to a private school is so much like <u>joining an expensive health club.</u>

Health club / private school. It's an a-la-carte world. That's how it works when you have money. Sign up and then choose the stuff you want. You're paying, so it's up to you.

How did you choose your club? When you looked at the splash page of its website, there was a babe who looked like a supermodel. Hey! I can look like a supermodel if I belong to this health club. Yes!

So then you needed a school for your son—you know, someplace that would whip him into shape to be a future Harvard man, or failing that, a Silicon Valley start-up billionaire.

Hey! Look at this private school! It has a terrific splash page: the boy in the photo knows geometry at age eleven, has well-developed executive function, can write beautifully, runs version 8.0 of Emotional Intelligence, and has done more backpacking than a Pacific Crest Trail celebrity. I am totally signing up my kid!

So you do. Terrific. Done! Score!

Though it is gauche to mention, you don't have to worry about who will show up as members at your club. They have an admissions policy. And a price tag. That is reassuring: only the kind of people you approve of will be there working out with you. And at the private school, if there is an undesirable student, you can always lobby to get him kicked out. You can say that he touched your son in an inappropriate way or that he takes up too many resources with his behavior issues.

And, of course, let us never forget: belonging to the club is a personal choice. You could go work out in the local public park or play pick-up basketball at the high school in the evenings. But you chose the club so that you could be consistent and get a good workout that would point you toward those ripped abs you know you deserve. Joining a club is the way to go. It's very personal. You're exercising a privileged choice. Works the same with a private school.

To start, there is a membership fee to join the club, like the tuition you pay at the school. You do have to sign up for a contract period of a year for both places, but you know in the back of your mind that you can always pull out and skip on the fees for the time remaining. Or demand a refund if you paid for time you did not yet use. Because you know they don't have the dough to come after you in court. Applies to the school too. You can drown them in legal fees.

Another thing, you know how you take a little gift to the staff at your club during the holidays? It's so they'll give you extra towels or let your friend in free or erase the fee if you forget to cancel a session with your personal trainer. You give them a tip—crisp bills—just as you do for your housecleaner or the guy who details your car. It's the nice gesture for people who serve you. You are a nice person. So, of course, you also tip the teacher, another person who serves you. It has nothing to do with buying good grades for your son during the season when teachers are writing high school recommendations.

You know how to work your scene at your exclusive, service-oriented, I-paid-good-money-for-this health club. A personal trainer is part of your club deal. The thing is, this guy has zero sense of humor. He expects you to work out five days a week and to increase your output of crunches and your treadmill time every week. He won't let you substitute the stair climber on slow mode for running, even though the treadmill is just not working for you. He doesn't understand that you need latte time and you have to connect with your peeps on your phone. What a drag. He expects you to treat this workout stuff like some enterprise from which you are going to extract a benefit. You end up kind of lying to him about what you're doing on the days he's not there. And you're cheating madly on the workout routine he gave you. But, hey, you're the one paying.

So cut to the school.

Like the club, the school offers that personal touch: one-on-one help for all students. You should not need to monitor stuff like homework or due dates. One-on-one teacher time by itself will guarantee your kid top grades.

But otherwise the school is pretty demanding, and it gets in the way. The school says students need to attend regularly because inconsistent attendance creates big holes in their learning. But you want to take your kid out to a fancy lunch on Wednesday. And you also really wanted to take the family to Hawaii in the middle of the semester because it's off-season. You like to go out to dinner, and that tends to cut into homework time.

Or the local team is pretty near getting to the World Series, and your business partner gave you his tickets for tonight, even though it's a Monday, and the kid has a test tomorrow.

Or you are really, really hungover from the Thursday night beers after work, and you cannot drive your kid to school this morning, so you let him sleep in. He won't get full value for his education today, but you're the one writing the checks, after all.

The teachers asked the parents to allow the students to record their own homework at the end of the day—that is, to write it out them-selves—so they will know what they need to do. However, you're in a big rush, and it's so much easier to snap a photo of it on your phone, and your son can look at the pic later. School rules forbid the use of a phone on campus, but since you're not a student, it's OK if you do it instead of him. Admittedly, he's not learning to do much for himself, but you're logging record time on the round trip to pick him up from school every day.

Your school isn't getting it that all the reading is just not working for your son. Just like your personal trainer doesn't get it that crunches are tough for you. The teacher asks for thirty minutes of leisure read-ing every night, assuring you the kid will get better at it with prac-tice. (Your trainer asks you to try doing twenty crunches week one, twenty-five week two, and then thirty week three, and he assures you that soon you'll be strong enough to do one hundred!) But that teacher doesn't take into account how hard it is to learn something new. And your trainer already has great abs. So both the teacher and the trainer are out of their minds. You just lie about doing the crunches, and your son learns to lie too. Who will ever know, after all? You both just play on your computers in the evening. So much more enjoyable. You can get movies for all the books the kid is assigned to read, anyway. He'll know the plots and can sort of fake the rest.

Then it's Monday again. You really don't like doing that workout with the trainer on Mondays. The weekend's been exhausting: parties and drinking and sleeping odd hours. In fact, you know for sure that while you were busy having fun, your son was booking major hours in online gaming, in addition to the two overnights he had with his buddies, and he, too, is pretty glassy-eyed come Monday morning.

But, hey, you send him to school. So what that he can't keep his eyes open. He's there, isn't he? He'll be fine.

And you can leave a message for your trainer and pretend you have an important client meeting and can't make the Monday workout.

The trainer works for you, after all.

Like the teachers do.

3

Rescuing Kids from Digital Isolation and Gaming the System

Our teenagers, and especially adolescent girls, are struggling. Their lives delineated by the explosion in communication through social media, they stand on the front lines of a cultural shift—even greater and more widespread than the one that occurred five hundred years ago with the invention of the printing press—that is dismantling long-held beliefs and values. It is an accelerating, undisciplined revolution. Teens live much of their lives in a world of digital isolation. Though many tout "connectedness" as overwhelmingly positive, the most fragile members of society—inexperienced and immature adolescents—are at tremendous risk of being victims rather than beneficiaries. We have an addiction problem on our hands.

Every kid is affected in some way. The overall statistical trends describing psychological well-being and social cohesion show up clearly in the day to day details under a teacher's nose. There is trouble brewing and private school students are not immune.

Observing as a veteran teacher, I see a generation of teens losing their way. They lead distracted, fragmented lives in which their sense of self and their moral compasses are beginning to drift under the onslaught of forces divorced from family and community. In the unfiltered digital world, the values celebrated are money, celebrity, gaming the system, getting ahead at whatever cost. The measure of success and status among teenagers has become a person's on-line persona, not the reflection from the eyes of a flesh-and-blood person standing before him or her.

The challenge for teachers and parents is to mediate this cultural shift and help adolescents keep to their true north. There is a bar-rage of boundary-free information all around them. Adolescents today must negotiate slippery terrain in the digital world where falsehood and fact slide past each other, accumulating in layers of revelation and deception.

Teenagers need adult guidance to understand the far more sig-nificant development of personal character, which is honed day to day in interactions, in person, with other people. It matters greatly among people living side by side if someone becomes known as the one who never returns a loan, the one who won't share, the one who tells lies when it is convenient, the one who discards friendships to gain personal advantage. Social media does not offer this feedback. Face-to-face intervention by adults is critical to help young people maintain the time-tested values that underpin our society. A school classroom provides solid ground for this work.

Researchers studying young people across the United States are now releasing the latest data on teen well-being. Their findings reflect the changes I have observed informally among my stu-dents over the past decade. The figures are alarming. In her 2017 book, *iGen: Why Today's Super-Connected Kids Are Growing Up*

Less Rebellious, More Tolerant, Less Happy—and Completely Unprepared for Adulthood, Jean M. Twenge, PhD, professor of psychology at San Diego State University, analyzed a massive nationwide survey administered by the Centers for Disease Control and Prevention. The survey was called Youth Risk Behavior Surveillance System, 1999-2015. In her book, Twenge reports, "Feeling sad or hopeless reached all-time highs (since 1999) in 2015 for girls, as did planning suicide, attempting suicide, and being injured in a suicide attempt. After declining during the 2000s, these suicide risk factors began to rise again after 2009."[1] The California Healthy Kids Survey results from a 2009–2010 poll of about 300,000 students found that 18 percent had contemplated suicide. Both studies concluded that for girls, suicide rates increased at a rate 1.5 times faster than the rate for boys.[2]

When suicide rates in girls aged ten to fourteen began to climb sharply in 1999, the American Psychiatric Association (APA) first suggested this jump could have been provoked by new FDA warnings that year on antidepressants such as Zoloft that were being linked to teenage suicides; this may have dissuaded doctors from prescribing them to teenagers. Another APA hypothesis pointed to the increasingly early onset of puberty among girls, now averaging around eleven years old, which could be causing the increase.[3] But all of these studies cover a period during which social media began to dominate the lives of teens: 24/7 connection, first through email, and then instant messaging and texting. I suspect a connection between the deterioration in the mental health of some of these vulnerable youth and their immersion in social media.

Consider a classic image of young teenage girls socializing: two girls sitting on the bed in one girl's bedroom, cross-legged, facing each other, slouched over long hair that drapes their faces, chipping at their nail polish or looking for split ends. They talk, laugh, snap at each other, sigh, moan, giggle. To an outsider, the conversation is content-less, but the girls are talking their own secret code and sharing intimacies with each other. They look into each other's eyes at certain moments, touch (or kick!) each other, hop up, try on clothes or makeup, all the while talking incessantly. The phone may ring, and one girl will talk while the other monitors or contributes to the conversation as well. Afterward, the two girls will dissect the contents of the phone call and share impressions. They are sharing, fact checking, and reality checking, while also reassuring or challenging each other, all of which is essential to high-caliber social interaction.

Fast forward a few years, and we find another indelible scene: the girls are now older but are still relating to each other in essentially the same intimate manner. The issues the fifteen- to nineteen-year-olds share with each other have more serious consequences: sex, alcohol, drugs, driving, scrapes with the law, pregnancy, getting into college. I think of the scene in the movie *Grease* in which a group of girlfriends quiz Sandy about her summer love affair with Danny, and in a split-screen parallel, some buddies grill Danny as well. In both scenes, the girl and the boy exaggerate their summer escapades, but they are doing so in person, in front of their friends. Eye contact, body language, the intimacy of the group's shared history all inform the telling of the tales. The content gets subtly fact checked, reality checked, challenged, or accepted at face value.

Things are changing now. The United States today is a material world where we are immersed in narcissistic behaviors, pop stars or reality TV celebrities are lionized, the household debt rate is ballooning. Everyone has a device in hand at every moment.

According to the Pew Research Center, 92 percent of teenagers aged thirteen to seventeen go online daily, and of those, 56 percent report online activity several times every day. Teenage girls dominate in the use of social media.[4] Communications from strangers or friends are indiscriminately invited or delivered as attacks. That teenagers, especially girls, should suffer under this onslaught is no surprise.

Teenagers are in a developmental phase in which they are intensely outer directed. Under the influence of hormones, their bodies are changing constantly. They are in a period of rapid intellectual and physical growth. Relationships with peers are of primary importance, while separation from or rebellion against parents is accelerating. Dr. Frances E. Jensen, in her 2015 book, *The Teenage Brain*, described attributes of the teenage brain that contribute to poor impulse control—which, for teenagers, results in a diminished ability to evaluate the wisdom of any potential act before carrying it out. They are reactive and impulsive.[5] And they are connected all the time.

Teenagers' devices are online around the clock, delivering non-parallel and asynchronous communications. There are no boundaries of any sort: the communications are constant, coming from all directions, benign as well as hostile, and impossible to defend against. Coordinating large groups of people to communicate on a single topic is easily realized through social media. It can launch a political uprising or protest march, or it might also be described as mob behavior, as reported in the *San Francisco Chronicle* on April 23, 2016: a mother was publicly shamed by thousands of strangers on Facebook for being a bad parent. Again, referring to the California Healthy Kids Survey 2009–2010, it was reported that 37 percent of students who had contemplated suicide were also the victims of cyber bullying, as compared to 18 percent of their peers.

Our personal exposure to intrusions from outside ourselves is at an all-time peak. There are almost no protections available, and people can't be held accountable for egregious behavior. Politeness and civility are foreign concepts.

Adolescents, like all human beings, need social connection for basic survival. Yet over the past twenty years, as parents' fears have heightened (the streets are no longer safe, roaming the neighborhood is not safe), adolescents have been led inside for their leisure. There they find computers and phones and lots of time to reach out. Though isolated in the physical sense, kids are constantly connected in the digital world, with no safeguards.

If teens increasingly experience the world through social media, it is not surprising that the least robust among them will suffer deteriorating mental health. Communication via social media isn't brokered by the same rules that are in play when the two girls sit opposite each other on the bed, nor when groups of friends are sharing stories face to face in a group. In real life, society uses controls to mitigate the dangers in arenas where teenagers are not yet capable of negotiating on their own: alcohol consumption, licenses to drive, access to illegal drugs, sexual activity. Yet this most potent mental health weapon, social media, has no breathalyzers, no seat belts, no urine tests. Disembodied communications in the digital world don't get passed through the essential filters that in-person human contact provides: eye contact, facial expressions, the empathy generated by the human presence of another warm body. There is no veracity check available, no "reading the situation" before acting, no sense of a human soul on the receiving end.

If you drop a girl, unprepared, into the Mojave Desert without food and water, will she survive? No. If you drop someone into the blips and bleeps of a digital community with no "environmental protections," it is reasonable to suspect she will not thrive either.

If girls aged ten to fourteen continue to be subjected to the incessant onslaughts delivered through their devices (their primary mode of social contact), the suicide rate will surely continue to climb. We face a challenge to use those opportunities we do have to shepherd our children past these dangers, if they are to arrive unscathed into adulthood.

The hours spent at school can make the difference. There, adult mentors, teachers, can offer guidance, sane limits, wholesome models for balance, restraint, community values.

In a typical school, students are assembled in classes of about twenty kids or more. There is a pervasive presence of technology, from the surreptitious use of cell phones to the increasingly ubiquitous use of screens of all sorts for every facet of the lessons. Schools place emphasis on test scores and achieving high GPAs. Students are immersed in a system of relentless competitive academics, and in order to survive, they resort to dealing and negotiating, bluffing and obfuscating, to outwit teachers and the system.

Frustrated at the prevalent ineffectiveness of most schools for teenagers, I designed a new model. The design turns away from several characteristics of contemporary schools and instead focuses on prioritizing the creation of strong relationships among students and teachers in small groups. No one functions optimally in a pack of twenty to thirty other individuals, so it is curious that we attempt to educate our young people in large groups. Instead, in a group of about twelve people, it is possible to focus on relevant, meaningful learning as well as the goal of having each person—student and teacher alike—contribute his or her best to the team. The underlying principles are community and collaboration: teachers and students cooperate in an environment of mutual compassion and respect, positive mind-set, and hard work.

This model emerged from my own experiences, as well as those of colleagues, in the classroom over almost thirty years. It seeks to address what could be termed a consumer-economics approach to school that has become the norm in middle and high schools. In the current climate, the student "pays" (sits in class, generates paper, and so on) and the teacher "delivers goods" (grades, recommendations). Parents get involved in the transactions by trying to bargain with or pressure teachers and administrators to enroll their students in more desirable classes or to obtain assignments for their students that will yield higher grades. Teachers participate by trimming and standardizing class content so that they can quantify it accurately and therefore defend that they have delivered the goods that had been paid for.

Though this portrayal seems stark and cynical, these basic assumptions underlie much of what transpires in typical classrooms. Students come to class seeking "credit" for their work and are deeply suspicious of being asked to do something for which they will not receive a grade. Consider the questions that teachers hear all the time:

"Will this be on the test?"
"Do I need to know this information?"
"I wrote the wrong answer on the test, but can I still get credit?"
"How much credit do I lose if I don't do this assignment?"

Students typically explain that they want good grades "so they can get into a good high school, and then a good college, and then get a good job." Or they decide to do community service or participate in an extracurricular activity "because it will look good on high school applications."

It is disheartening that very rarely is there a conversation about wanting to learn about the world or figure out how to make a contribution. Students are, as Denise Clark Pope describes it, "doing school."[6] Teachers are locked into the system as well, dreading the metrics of evaluation and day after day confronting a lack of curiosity or deep thinking among students—who are, instead, functioning in an environment of deal making, trying to game a system that pits teachers against students.

At the start, when we introduced a new school model, we had to work hard to convince students to adopt a different vision and attitude about school. Our goal was to broaden their curiosity about the world, to improve their ability to think critically, to help them find a path for making their lives matter in the larger scheme. This is a radically new concept for most adolescents. As teachers, our strongest tools are to be living models of commitment to lifelong learning and overcoming personal challenges, while embracing meaningful, challenging work. Students are initially reluctant to do work for which they will receive no "payment" in grades, such as investing in classroom discussion, reading extra material outside class, listening to public radio news analyses, or consulting a good newspaper. Likewise, students are astonished to be shown that the English teacher can do higher math, that the biology teacher knows poetry, that the adults follow workout routines to stay fit, that teachers also have to study world geography to follow international news intelligently.

A window does open, nevertheless. After the initial resistance and disbelief, students almost always embrace this different way of regarding school and education. It is a huge relief, in fact, to be freed of what is essentially an adversarial system, with students purchasing favor from teachers, and teachers standing in judgment of students. Instead, students and teachers together unleash curiosity, explore new ideas, hone an understanding of the world. Teachers are not set up as experts, and students are not diminished as mere recipients of information. This model of cooperative group learning dismantles the "us versus them" dynamic that fuels anxiety and stress.

This better educational context, one that stimulates authentic learning and the acquisition of broad competency, is shaped by the culture of the school. Several core ideas establish the foundation. Relationships come first: individuals (students and teachers) feel known, safe, and valued. The fundamentals of working toward consensus underpin these relationships. The group's well-being is superior to any one person's advantage, and being accountable to commitments is the central theme. There is no teacher-student hierarchy: hard work, hard play, and lifelong learning are practices everyone embraces.

Successful learning depends on an emotional underpinning. What we ask students to learn must be highly relevant—in fact, inspiringly relevant and satisfyingly challenging—or it will not interest a teenager.

Our students would say that we ask everything of them, that we push them to their limits. One of my students characterized my teaching as "a river, unrelenting," and then he grinned widely. I tell them relentlessly that they can give more than they think they can give, and I will guide them, support them, and keep up the pressure. So as they struggle and work harder than they ever have, they go further than they imagined possible.

I like to remember Nadia, who pushed through the barriers of her extreme dyslexia at age thirteen and captured the writing award that year. I think of Briana, who turned her adolescent rebellion and apathy into an award in the county speech tournament with the brilliantly sarcastic "How to Get a Date." I ask a lot of my students but never at a distance. We work together. Our efforts are interspersed with hard play and lots of humor—irreverent, kooky, silly, immature teenage humor.

Teenagers watch adults to learn how to be in the world. A teacher can show students that learning does not stop at the classroom door. We have dropped everything to organize an impromptu excursion to the peak of Mt. Tamalpais on the day it snowed—knowing how to make a well-turned snowball is a life skill. I have worked one on one with my students after school and at night, on the phone or online, as they needed it. The message: teachers use their brains even when they are not standing in the classroom.

As teachers, we try our best to model lifelong learning around the clock, at the beach on weekends, in the desert for stretches during vacations and summers. The reluctant public speakers surprise me by wanting to recite Edna St. Vincent Millay by the campfire in the middle of the wilderness. The ones who hate English are thrilled to scream out the scientific names of lizards that skitter by as we bump along wilderness roads. The bad boy who is just scraping by academically is stoically happy to slog slowly, painfully up the side of

9,700-foot Mt. Tallac to claim the summit—and afterward to demonstrate his prowess at roasting bagels over a camp stove while we debate the idea of individual freedom. I believe that teaching happens everywhere and that the "teachable moment" is to be honored. My greatest joy is to get a few of them out in the desert for "road school," where learning can take on the tinge of survival instinct: we reckon GPS coordinates, test rock climbing holds, and learn problem solving via the challenges of auto mechanics when we find ourselves miles from a service station. Learning is never ending and as essential to well-being as water and air.

The most effective teachers ask for the best and hold the line. They model the joy of intellectual engagement. Studying the history of ancient Africa becomes compelling as we talk about the current struggles in Sudan and Nigeria, keep up with the issues in the news, or write letters to Amnesty International. Teachers still have things to learn, just as the students do. We need to know the fundamentals of Islam and analyze the current popular perversions of the original message, so I invite a Palestinian refugee couple to speak to the class for a morning. Studying medieval Japan is the perfect moment for students to take part in a traditional tea ceremony and experience one kind of meditative practice. There is no moment like the present—for example, at a rest stop along Interstate 5 en route to the mountains—for students to sit with each other and struggle with the breakdowns that occur when they forget the spirit of cooperation that we have practiced over and over in class meetings. I believe in letting students stumble and find their own solutions, with ever-present guidance but without adults rescuing them.

I love teaching because I love learning, and I love teenagers because they are courageous and alive, willing to change. If teachers can work to be authentic, willing to take risks and stay open to change, teenagers will follow.

The heart of the national conversation about education today is why our schools are failing, how to design better schools, what we need in education reform. I hear it at the micro level from parents of middle schoolers who are searching for the best fit in a high school for their children. But there is a difference in perspective between parents and professional educators.

It seems that almost always the conversation with parents begins with their saying they want their kid to love learning and to enjoy school. The next thing they say is that they want a school that will allow their child to "pursue his passion." While both motivations seem well intentioned and laudable, they are misdirected and, in fact, counterproductive to ensuring a solid education for their children.

First, we have to acknowledge the powerful force of what my colleagues call the "kid lobby." Anyone who has been a parent (or an attentive teacher, for that matter) has experienced the ferocious power of the kid lobby. Children advocating for fun and comfort can be and usually are relentless in their efforts to get what they want. The pleasure principle is the chief catalyst in the behavior of most people until well into their midteens. As one of my more articulate thirteen-year-old students once put it to me, "I have always been able to wear down the adults around me to get what I want, so why would I think you can resist me?"

Here's what adolescents want: to do what they love to do, to do what they are good at doing, to relax a lot, to be free of adult nagging (which adults call evaluation), to stay comfortable. Sometimes—in fact, often—parents characterize this as the student's "passion."

Here is what it takes to grow into a clear-thinking, well-informed, effective, and successful adult: a reasonably solid and serious control of knowledge across the disciplines (above the *Wikipedia* level), tolerance for pursuing work that is difficult or not intrinsically of great personal interest, persistence to keep going despite frustrations and setbacks, and discipline to work hard every day and according to a consistent rhythm that moves projects forward.

Persistence, tolerance, purpose, and discipline—this is not what young people think they want from school, but it is what they need. Implementing a plan to teach these qualities provokes significant resistance at first, but teenagers can and almost always do embrace it. Parents are slower to come around. Learning is not "fun" 100 percent of the time, but real learning is astonishingly rewarding and addictive.

4

Stress as a Dirty Word

A couple of years ago, as I was trying to figure out where teen education had gone off track, I started to keep a journal of my days at school. An entry from a typical day on the front lines is sobering but revealing.

According to the journal, I had yet another depressing, frustrating—no, pulling-my-hair-out—day teaching my affluent, coddled middle school students. The day before, we had spent an hour learning Central America geography. We recited a cute mnemonic to memorize the countries—"My Baby Gorilla Eats Hotdogs, not Cocoa Puffs,"—and watched, then sang along with a YouTube rap video presenting the countries and capitals from Mexico south to Panama, repeating the process *several times*. Catchy. We all hummed the tune the rest of the day. Kids were given blank maps so that they could fill in the countries' names and the capital cities. We covered just about every learning style there is and had fun at it, and the kids were told there would be a quiz on the following day on what we had covered. There were twenty-eight geographic labels that we had identified and placed on the map. On the day of the quiz, students had to label any ten locations to earn an A. Three-quarters of the students scored 50 percent or lower on the quiz!

Later in the day, students were to present dramatic pieces they had been assigned *three weeks earlier* to memorize for the upcoming speech tournament. Only a quarter of the students completed that assignment.

On Tuesday, I gave a quiz on the material we had read aloud together and discussed in class on Monday in world history. We previewed the lesson as a group, noting the time line, the key terms, and the reading focus. Students took turns reading aloud. We discussed the lesson's questions. We placed the important dates on the classroom's time-line display, each student climbing a chair to affix a date to the Velcro chart. I asked them to review their reading for a quiz Tuesday. Two-thirds of the students failed Tuesday's quiz (with scores of 20 percent to 40 percent).

These are "smart" kids. They have involved, successful parents. It did not used to be this way.

I think the culprit is stress—a lack of stress. These students, in contrast to my students of even ten years ago, live in a world made soft and comfy and easy by their wealthy parents. It is too far for Tad to ride his bike one mile to school with his fat history book in his backpack. Jen and Kasey go out to a fancy French café and drop $40 for an after-school snack, while they text their friends on their $650 smartphones. Parents consider homework to be an unfair burden. When we ask the kids to play tennis in PE, they all want to have a break after thirty minutes. They don't pack their own lunches. They don't use alarm clocks. They don't do chores. They are not even required to take a daily shower. They know all of the finest restaurants in town because they go there often. They vacation at beach clubs.

No wonder the notion of straining to learn something is foreign to these kids. They have learned that if something is uncomfortable, they should stop trying. They know that if they complain enough about how hard something is, their parents will not be able to stand their pain, so they will be rescued. If education—if anything at all— is not fun, then they are not interested. Here's what is OK: gourmet food, videos on the internet, soft beds and couches, manicures and massages, four-star hotels on Daddy's dime, fancy electronics, fancy cars. Here's what is dumb: studying anything to learn it solidly, being really smart on a subject, true competence won through painful practice and repetition.

We have created a generation of children who are the embodiment of the caterpillar, which is cut from its chrysalis without having to struggle or strengthen its wings to break free. The newly hatched butterfly is too weak to fly. Our kids are too weak to thrive.

No wonder there's a trend toward personalized "a la carte" educational outfits such as Fusion Academy. At such places, a student sits one on one with a single adult, who spoons learning into the kid's mind. The adult shovels it in; the kid passively accepts it. There is no period of independent, solo practice that follows, which would allow for the learning to digest and assimilate at a deeper level. These "fast ed" places consider homework another dirty word. Too stressful on the parents, too stressful on the kids. Someone might get strong and really learn with all that pain! Just drop by the fast-ed shop when you "feel like learning" or "it suits you," and you, too, can get a little skim of education to set you up for life.

5

There's an App for That

Because my mother died when I was just seven, my four siblings and I were raised through our formative years largely by local country women. My widowed father needed what today we would call childcare; in those days, he needed "a woman to do for him," as my grandmother put it. (The term *nanny* had not yet filtered down to the middle classes.) Over the course of five years, until my father remarried, we children were placed in the competent hands of a few different hardworking women: Mrs. Jones, Mrs. Brant, and Mrs. Schoch. I gained lifelong inspiration from those minimally educated women. They knew how to work their brains to make do in hard times, using ingenuity, inventiveness, and problem solving. We need that inspiration today. In fact, we would hire those women to design apps.

Originally, I was embarrassed by the profound influence these capable women had on me. They could make the proverbial silk out of any sow's ear, but I could not appreciate their genius. This was the 1950s, and we in postwar America were learning to love buying power and the quick, easy conveniences of laborsaving inventions, such as TV dinners and wrinkle-free polyester. It was no longer stylish to do things ourselves the hard way.

So in the fourth grade, I came home one day and announced I needed to make a clock face from a paper plate for the next day's learn-to-tell-time lesson at school. With glee, I anticipated getting Mrs. Schoch to take me downtown to the dime store to buy paper fasteners (called brads), essential for holding the clock hands tightly against the paper plate.

Nothing doing! Shopping was not in Mrs. Schoch's arsenal of remedies for any situation whatsoever. Instead, she showed me how to use two buttons from my father's worn-out shirt. She threaded them together, one on either side of the paper plate, and they efficiently held secure the arms of my practice clock face. I was thoroughly disappointed at her inventing a clever solution instead of taking me to the dime store; moreover, I was so ashamed of her work-around that I tried to hide my clock from classmates the next day at school. It worked perfectly, however, and much later I would secretly admit to myself that she was pretty much a genius.

Today, there'd be an app for both clock construction and the learn-to-tell-time lesson. Such an impoverishing turn of events! Computers can do so much for us now that we've turned over a lot of our human potential and have abdicated our learning.

Today, I take kids out stargazing at night, and they don't want to lie on their backs and try to figure out the patterns in the blackness overhead. They just want to hold up a cell phone and have the app tell them what to see. I have lunch with my students, and they don't want to chat, not even about themselves; they want to Instagram photos of the food to their friends across the country. I ask a kid on the school trip to read the road signs and direct me to our next turn, but he is busy talking to Siri and misses the giant artichoke of Castroville as we whiz by. All of these lost opportunities to experience, to feel in control of the world, to be competent and ingenious, just by using their own brainpower.

There's an app for just about everything. You don't have to bother to learn or take time to master skills. You can abdicate control of so many facets of your life to the machine if you want to.

The irony is that technology in education was touted as one of the great tools for teaching our kids to be creative, work cooperatively, and pool their geniuses. I see the opposite occurring in the classroom. Given that they have a shortcut at hand, why would kids plod the long way toward solutions? Brainstorming ideas with a classmate is cumbersome, time consuming, and often messy. Of course, the answer is that by exploring, trying out ideas, thinking of alternative approaches, and collaborating with each other in person, we can come up with new solutions to old problems. To the extent that we teach young people to go to an app and take some programmer's word for it, we hamstring the mother of invention—necessity. We are suffocating the creative impulse.

Students cannot tell me how to drive to their homes to pick them up. An app, not their own bodies, informs them whether they have exercised enough on a given day. Facebook reminds people about Grandma's birthday and even generates a digital greeting to her without requiring anyone to invest in personal inspiration. I no longer use my well-worn wildflowers book, the one with the dog-eared pages covered in scrawls, the one telling me when and where I saw a particular plant—I use the app and instantly forget. We look at the weather app instead of checking outside the window. The tourists don't know a thing about Berlin but just follow the app, heading from monument to monument. You don't even have to keep track of your belongings because there's an app to locate them when you lose them. The school can send you a video of your kid working in the classroom, so you needn't bother your darling in the evening with a loving question, "How was your day, honey?" An app can tell you where your teenager is on his date, so you may as well be living in his hip pocket, you have robbed him of so much of his privacy. It is shocking and sad how much independence we have given away.

This practice of abdication comes at a price.

Laborsaving programs surely are a blessing, but not if we become so enthralled that we rob ourselves of agency. An app can lay out solutions to algebra problems so that students can get the "right" answer, despite their lack of understanding. Google Translate relieves us of having to master verb tenses in Spanish, so we manipulate the language in a rote manner without real comprehension. We dial up *Wikipedia* factoids but don't learn historical context. The teenage store clerk can't do simple math, so he has to get out his phone to use the calculator.

Who dares try a new restaurant without Yelp? Mentally calculate a tip? Visit a real doctor instead of self-diagnosing by using the internet? Use a map of any sort instead of listening to route guidance in the car? Sing your baby to sleep at night? Allow yourself to be bored to see what you come up with?

Nah, just get the app. Everyone with the nice, same, uniform apps.

6

Hijacking Human Potential in Learning: Technology Run Amok

It all began innocently enough. Harried parents in the 1980s discovered the beatific balm of the video machine for helping toddlers and young kids settle down, so the adults at least could have a conversation. While dinner was cooking, laundry was getting folded, and bills were being paid, there could be a moment of peace. A quick peek into the family room would reveal kids sprawled contentedly on the carpet, transfixed by the screen. Reliably, grown-ups could enjoy thirty minutes of sanity before one segment of cartoons played out. Parents could quantify their freedom in program segments. It was bliss.

The kids did look a little drugged, though, drooling or sucking thumbs in rapt attention. If you stood back and considered the scene, it was a little creepy—but sanity preserving and lifesaving. And the kids liked it. Soon, they were yammering for it.

A few years later came the proliferation of personal computers in the home. Parents could give their kids access to the family computer, and life was even better. No need to go change the videos in the machine. The kid would be occupied for a long time just waiting for the landline-based internet connection to engage. OK, so maybe parents did discover their sixth grader was getting up before them on Saturday mornings to look at the "kitty" sites online. But there was the salve of parental controls, which everyone firmly believed would safeguard the darlings. And, anyway, how different was the internet than TV?

Fast forward. The Apple-computers-for-every-school movement. The advent of the laptop. Then the wired classroom, and the entire school linked by email. Internet availability in the library, and then for every teacher, and soon for any student lucky enough to have his mom's laptop at school. There followed an almost religious fervor for providing a laptop to every single student. Homework posted online. Internet on the school buses. Apps for math lessons. And on and on. Now, there were a few glitches about controlling access to adult content, but the kids seemed to weather the exposure OK.

I taught in middle schools throughout this entire revolution. I watched classrooms and education fundamentally change in response to digital dominance. It was dramatic but often not so positive as advertised.

Absolutely sobering are the effects on students, the kids, that I have witnessed in person. Progress always exacts a price, but few people are tracking just what that price has been to the adolescents on the front lines.

Scene: last week after school, in the library of a pricey private high school. It's the homework help period. Freshmen, sophomores, and juniors have gathered to complete their assignments in a quiet place where resource teachers are available to offer assistance. The parents insist on this extra service, their students working under adult supervision. The kids are seated along the tables, their laptops open, silently tapping in isolation. A cursory glance tells nothing, but a closer look reveals that the teenagers also have their phones in their laps, open to first-person shooter games, or Snapchat, or Instagram, or just ubiquitous, incessant text messaging. Every student in the place is doubly wired and multitasking. The adult supervisors in the room are mere ephemera, barely registered. What's happening on the screen, especially that little screen, is more real than reality. And they are all transfixed.

Scene: an even fancier, more exclusive private high school's English class, Tuesday afternoon, 2:00 p.m. The discussion in progress is about last night's reading from Kafka's *The Castle*. Tough stuff that needs a lot of chewing. Desks are arranged in the narrow room, four abreast. At the start of class, Linda, a girl sitting near the back, had her hand up for every question. She made lively contributions, and the teacher beamed. Since then, the teacher has turned his attention to other students, encouraging them to contribute as much as Linda has. Just what Linda wanted, because now she is ignored and can attend to the phone in her lap. She's talking to friends but also scanning her math problems into a handy app that will spit out step-by-step solutions. She can copy these onto her homework sheet. So efficient, all that she is accomplishing in English class!

Since the mid-1990s, I have noticed enormous changes in my teenage students as they have been subjected to the impacts of technology saturation. I see a pronouncedly diminished capacity for sustained reading of print material, especially books. Even my most accomplished middle school students in the last few years began to neglect print reading and did not manage to comply with the one-book-a-month leisure reading assignment. This impinged on the caliber of books I could successfully assign for class reading. In 1996, for example, every two days I could assign thirty pages of a book that had won, say, the top literary award for young adult fiction. I could expect students to read, comprehend, and complete ten questions on the assignment. Today, that would be considered fairly onerous.

In the year 2000, I would assign the reading of a fifteen-page short story (often a classic or the caliber of *The New Yorker* magazine) plus the writing of a related five-hundred-word essay every week, and that in addition to requesting students to read and digest thirty pages of dense social studies content. I still have records of those lesson plans and the related papers students turned in, but my most recent students could not handle that load of reading.

Similar observation: the three hundred volumes of contemporary young adult fiction that we assembled in our middle school library gathered dust for two years. Five years ago, the books flew off the shelves. Kids were still reading nightly, even classics. On class trips, we could call a DEAR (drop everything and read) period of thirty minutes, and reliably we would find that every student could sustain focus the entire time. No more. Today, half of my students would be exhausted and fidgety after fifteen minutes, and this would be reading material of their own choosing. They'd want their phones—or any screen—for relief.

Basic practical skills have withered. Students struggle to manipulate a print dictionary (or an alphabetical listing of any sort of information), finding it cumbersome to make their way efficiently around the ABCs. I know this because every year, we used to have fun with "dictionary races" in English class to sharpen these skills. Now, students no longer find those races amusing because they are too difficult. Likewise, it is too difficult to read an analog clock or use a wall calendar (print). The sequencing skills built through print book reading are no longer strongly in place. This then impinges on the ability to comprehend a time line in history. Map-reading skills have withered. Ten years ago, we used to play a map game in the classroom: one student would draw a map to go from school to home, and then the other students would try to figure out where the map drawer lived. Or we'd do a treasure hunt to find a stash of candy: students would need to follow written directions (go east, go west, go twenty yards, and so on) and a paper map to find their way across the school campus and to the treasure pile. These games are much trickier for students today.

Many are baffled with the task of addressing an envelope because they no longer understand the system of tiered information defining locations: person, house number, street name, town name, state name. Ask many adolescents to tell you their parents' phone numbers, and they cannot do it. They rely on their devices. Making sense of the physical world and its organization (for instance, country, state, county, city, neighborhood) has eroded among all the facts floating free in the digital universe.

Time management and organization skills have suffered. On a computer, as we all know, a user needs to adhere to a strong organization system in order to store and retrieve documents efficiently. All of us have experienced losing something in the digital haze. But for adolescents who are still developing sequencing and sorting skills, digital format is a huge hazard. They remain in the developmental stage of needing tangible handles to be reliably successful as they manipulate items, access them, and then save them for later retrieval.

Today, students turn in papers with big chunks of text either missing or copied out twice. They click through a spelling- and grammar-check program without evaluating the choices offered, so papers are littered with errors. A colleague who teaches English in the local public high school experiences similar difficulties. Like many contemporary teachers, she focuses on the "process" of writing, having students craft multiple drafts of a given paper. But lacking a physical paper trail for the drafts not only makes it very difficult for anyone to track the evolution of a student's thesis as it develops over time, but also makes it challenging to verify that a finished product is truly the student's own work.

With multiple distractions yammering for attention all the time, adolescents' ability to manage time has been significantly impaired. Few tasks can be initiated and completed without multiple interruptions from phones, messaging apps on the computer, pop-ups from the internet, and so on. I watch students fritter away class time allotted to beginning or completing a homework assignment. They open and close windows, check the calendar, view the clock, monitor emails. They are lost in the flashing light of the screen.

Students' grasp of spelling and writing conventions is a significant casualty of computer-based education. In fact, they pretty much no longer believe that either matters. Hence, written language skills have become impoverished. The abbreviations and truncated slang from messaging apps show up in school assignments: "If u read washingtons farewell address u can understand what i did. He was worried about the country having 2 many alliances with foreign countries."

Students' ability to take handwritten notes has eroded, yet word-processed note taking does not work as an adequate substitute: pop-up notices of spelling errors, grammar tips, and so on, make concentrated and efficient note taking on a computer very difficult. For a majority of young people, handwriting skills in general have weakened. For most of my students, writing a formal eight-line thank you note is a time-consuming and frustrating task.

Meanwhile, in science class, it is obsolete to require students to copy by hand color diagrams of, say, a plant cell or a human heart. Lost are the kinesthetic benefits of sketching that are so integral to learning complicated organic structures such as these. Students capture diagrams and lecture points the teacher has written on the smart board, or they download digital diagrams and substitute passive mouse clicks for active learning techniques. Meanwhile, across the hall in Spanish class, few students create physical paper flash cards for studying vocabulary. They use computer-generated versions and never get practice writing out words, noting and using correct spelling as they go along.

My students today struggle with tasks for which elementary mathematics is needed. Calculators have been in the hands of school kids for a couple of decades. Now they are ubiquitous on both computers and phones. Consequently, few students can do calculations quickly and accurately in their heads, not even the math whizzes. This might seem to be an old-fashioned skill, until it plays out in real life, such as when I take students on outdoor education trips. In planning for the trip, we try estimating what we will need to buy at the grocery store. For instance, at a quarter pound per person, how many one-and-a-half pound packages of hamburger will we need to feed twenty-eight people—about five or about ten? If we each need a gallon of liquids per day for hiking in the desert, about how many cases of seventeen-ounce bottles should we buy—ten, fifteen, twenty? Is it more economical to buy a group pass or pay individual admissions to the art museum for our group of ten students and two adults? And so on. Bereft of their phone calculators, many students are stymied by these everyday tasks, and we end up hungry people at the burger cookout or with six extra cases of Gatorade when we return from a camping trip.

We used to play a game of toss-and-catch in the classroom to practice multiplication facts. I had a cache of small balls labeled with math-fact problems. I would toss a ball to a student who would read the label (for example, "six times eight") and quickly answer (correctly, "forty-eight") and then toss the ball back to me. Then I'd toss "nine times seven" to someone else, and so on. I would challenge them to go through the entire basket of math balls faster and faster over several trials, and if they beat their record, everyone got a prize (fittingly, a Dum Dum lollipop). Students thought this was great fun, especially because of the ironic reward. But a few years ago, we had to stop playing the game, because joking about not being "dum dums" seemed kind of cruel, given that the students never could beat the record. Their mental math skills were too weak.

With online research dominating now, I have watched *Wikipedia* become the primary (and often the only) source of information consulted when students are assigned to quickly learn about a new topic. My colleagues in local high schools observe the same phenomenon. Students have lost a lot of their ability to evaluate the reliability of any particular source of information on the web, where all information is presented horizontally, without any sort of vetting.

And sorting through the results of an open web search is often confusing and time consuming. Everyone simply goes to *Wikipedia*.

Today's student is slightly baffled by a request to go to the brick and mortar library and talk to the reference librarian. Broad, deep investigations into any subject have become restricted and of poor quality. The concept of categorizing information in hierarchies of increasing detail and complexity is lost as today's student simply types a question into a search box. So if a student needs to investigate a complicated issue (or find information buried deep in the context of a topic), he gets nowhere. Two years ago, a student informed me there was nothing on the internet about the arguments for and against building desalination plants to solve California's water crisis. She was utterly stymied by the poverty of her skills and was incapable of teasing out facts relevant to her argument from articles on related topics. Researching the government's no-fly list, another student announced he had found the TSA site where all the names were listed. Of course, the place he had landed on was a hoax, but it had TSA in its title!

The effects spill over into the social realm in a pronounced way. Colleagues teaching in local high schools observe that students no longer chat with each other when they arrive early for a class. Kids are buried in cell phones instead of getting to know the people around them—the very people with whom they have been assigned to collaborate on group projects. Gone are the opportunities to make friends or even compare answers from last night's homework. In the car on field trips to museums or overnight camping trips, students clamor to play games on handheld devices or watch videos on phones. One parent complained to me that her son could not endure a three-hour car ride without a video game. At lunchtime, few students choose to pull out the chess sets or to laugh and joke over board games. On the local private high school campus, access is denied to sites such as Netflix because watching movies over the lunch break is against official school rules; however, enterprising and "techy" students simply defeat the blocking software in the computer lab and—voila!—each student is now hunched over his or her own tiny screen.

In the first few years of the computer revolution, my teaching colleagues and I embraced it. We encouraged every student to bring a laptop to school, sent assignments through email, and posted homework online. But we were forced to retreat. Students quickly discovered how to use the new tools to satiate their voracious adolescent appetites for amusement. They watched cartoons, searched for cute pictures of cats, copied whole website pages into documents and passed them off as their own writing ("saving time"), instant messaged each other in class, shopped online, or sent emails to their moms complaining that the teacher was being mean in class. They became adept at making up excuses for not doing their work by blaming technological glitches: "My internet went down, so I didn't get the homework assignment" or "My computer crashed, and I lost my document after I had completed the work" or "I did email it to you, and it must have gone into your spam filter." The perfect smoke screen.

First, we tried to keep control of the internet on campus by using passwords, but that soon proved too cumbersome, and students figured out the passwords anyway. Then we set up a rule that students needed to ask permission to go online at school. Again, we met failure. Loopholes abounded. Students' use of laptops to word process their answers to test questions likewise backfired, since they could not resist accessing stored notes on their machines. We tried having them trade and use each other's computers for tests, but slight differences in hardware and software meant that some kids lost half a test period trying to start a document and save it properly. Then there was all of the lost data. "Bad stuff happens" more than usual to teenagers working on computers.

Overriding all is the amount of distraction that technology interjects into the classroom as well as into study hall. The bright flashes, little chirps, expanding and collapsing windows, pop-up messages—it is too much for any but the most rigidly disciplined teenager to resist. Students disappear into a digital circus far more entertaining and colorful than real life. Parents would complain to us that Billy spent three hours on his homework last night, but in reality Billy had developed impressive reflexes for toggling from one screen to another as his mother walked into his room to check up on him.

Given an essay assignment in class, a thirteen-year-old boy can take ten minutes or more to open up a word processing program and begin a new document, what with all the temptations to choose font, format, header/no header, line spacing, and so on. I ask students to take notes on a history discussion, and the same thing occurs: I look out onto a sea of glowing Apple icons, no human eyes visible above the screens over which the kids are hunched, lovingly toggling between calendar and document, online dictionary and spell check, Ask Jeeves website and font style. They are so distant they don't even hear their names called in the discussion.

There is a very different feel from having students look at the board and copy notes by hand. A study at Princeton University in 2014 concluded that taking notes by hand was superior to word processing in terms of students' ability to recall key ideas. Professor Jonathan Zimmerman of the University of Pennsylvania Graduate School of Education maintains that the process of handwriting notes forces students to order information, but those using a computer are simply transcribing the words of the teacher without organizing the information hierarchically.[7]

In my classes, if we try to watch a video on the screen, inevitably we are interrupted by someone trying to enlarge the image, or increase the volume, or hit the pause button to ask about something he missed while he was jiggering with the buttons. It is a very different atmosphere when we listen intently to an audio recording minus any visuals. Teenagers have a tough time sorting through competing types of input to focus on the most important one for the task at hand.

Three years into the wholehearted adoption of a wired classroom, we teachers pulled back considerably. To the utter horror of our modern, plugged-in parents, we began suggesting students leave their laptops at home. We stopped using the online-access study program for vocabulary and went back to using paper workbooks and pencils. They had to think to answer the questions in the workbooks and to test their responses, because there were no happy sounds or exploding star icons to reward them for a mindless hunt-and-peck approach to the assignments. We limited the number of web resources a student could use for any research project and insisted everyone get a library card and go back to consulting the reference librarians. We ran every paper through a plagiarism-checking program and announced the results when we discovered forgeries. We no longer accepted "My computer crashed" or "I lost my document" as legitimate reasons to be excused for late assignments. Sounds Luddite-like, but the reality is that everything had spun out of control. Technology was compromising our ability to reach our students in a meaningful way. The realities notwithstanding, it is difficult to jump off the "wired school" bandwagon in a climate in which parents demand more and more technology and in which nonteacher reformers view it unquestioningly as the latest and greatest tool in education.

The scourge has spread beyond the classroom as well. Before digital saturation, we used to communicate with parents face to face, through handwritten notes or by telephone. I had never appreciated what an efficient filter that provided us. Parents got through to teachers with urgent or important messages, but the petty stuff just wasn't worth the effort: to show up at school, or to find paper and pen, or to wait for the teacher to wade through the voicemail message on the classroom phone and eventually call back.

Now, with instant communication at the fingertips of parents at every moment, we are subjected to every unvarnished detail of parental angst or lack of organization. Parents email and message us 24/7: wholesale complaints, changes of plan, reports of sobbing over homework, criticism of assignments, descriptions of family drama. They used to become furious if we did not respond promptly (during the school day, while teaching their children), so we were driven to put in place a new policy of responding only once a day and after school. Parents began demanding that we carry along satellite phones on outdoor education trips and email them every evening to assure them the students were still alive out there in the Sierra forest. They wanted us to send them the homework assignment Suzie had forgotten at school or to email us at noon to explain that Alex was operating without his medications today. Too often they blew off steam in angry emails sent long past midnight. In self-preservation, we had to turn off our devices. We felt under assault.

Today, I see adolescents tethered to their parents in ways that they (and their parents) would have found intolerable twenty years ago. Parents text kids constantly and encourage their children to do the same in return. I see fourteen-year-olds who feel uneasy about walking downtown without a cell phone for security. They consult their parents on all sorts of decisions for which they should be developing skills to be independent: What am I doing after school today? Where is my biology book? Should I buy this sweater or that one? Can you email the homework I forgot to print out?

Years ago, I ran an exciting and enlightening history exercise for my teenage students. In small Vermont towns, I dropped them off two by two, with a couple of bucks in their pockets, as well as paper and pencils. For the entire day, they had to gather the history of the location of their "drop off" and write up a little story about the people they had met and what they had learned. Without exception, the students had great fun, engaged with so many people (mostly elderly), gathered fascinating information, and made new friends. They felt empowered, emboldened, a part of something very real. Today, few parents could tolerate such freedom, and many students would feel at risk. The phantom security of a cell phone has impinged on an important phase of maturation for young people.

The wholesale worship of technology in education feels so similar to other trends that have come and gone in US education. The United States scrambled to catch up to Russia after the Sputnik launch in 1957. We produced a new teaching program called New Math, and it was broadly adopted. A whole generation of kids grew up unable to manipulate basic arithmetic and was rendered allergic to mathematics until that program was sacked around 1970. Then there was the "open education movement" (eventually abandoned by about the mid-1970s), which greatly deprived students, especially poor and disadvantaged ones, of attention to basic skills acquisition in elementary school. This led, in the 1980s, to an increased need for remedial classes in both high school and college.

A presidential commission in 1983 produced a national assessment of education in the United States. The report, titled *A Nation at Risk*, propelled the country into another fad to improve the caliber of math and science education. Then came the fervent embrace of a new protocol called the National Council of Teachers of Mathematics (NCTM) Standards in the 1990s that, for example, championed issuing calculators to young elementary students and abandoning rote learning of arithmetic. Predictably, too, this would lead to a movement toward accountability (and standardized testing nationwide) by the late 1990s. An invention called "whole language learning" impeded children's acquisition of strong reading skills and was ditched in the mid-1990s. In every case, we threw common sense out the door and abandoned pedagogical techniques that had worked faithfully for years. In their place, we embraced something new and flashy and cool.

Education fundamentally deals with disciplining and training a human mind. Everyone learns in a deeply personal way, and the best teaching will be delivered by a person who is responsive to the individual's needs. Compelling results from a recent study conducted by professors David DeSteno, Cynthia Breazeal, and Paul Harris were published in the journal *Frontiers in Human Neuroscience* and summarized in the *New York Times*. In the article, the authors discuss why educational technology has been a disappointment: "In our view...the designers of...technologies rely on an erroneous set of assumptions about how the mind learns. Yes, the human brain is an amazing information processor, but it evolved to take in, analyze and store information in a specific way: through social interaction."[8]

I see in the classroom what the researchers discovered in their experiments: person-to-person interaction is a superior way to teach.

I don't believe that "there is an app for everything." A blind devotion to technology and its laborsaving assistance is not conducive to the acquisition of deep understanding. We've allowed ourselves to become transfixed beyond all reason. I predict a backlash—I hope for one—and a return to a more measured approach, one that pairs technology thoughtfully and sparingly with flesh-and-blood teaching. There is no substitute for an attentive teacher working in focused rapport with students, making sure they're gaining a firm foundation in basic concepts.

We have run amok in our love for the machine, and it's time to rein ourselves in and use our brains.

7

Our Children Are Fragile Flowers: Bamboozled by the Kid Lobby

Kids are mirror reflections of the insecurities, worries, and prejudices they observe in older people, especially their parents. They are also adept at spotting loopholes and wheedling their way into chinks in adult armor.

In today's climate of fearfulness about the future—for our society, for the very planet—we are becoming increasingly gullible and astonishingly susceptible to false news or shrill alarms spread through social media. For many parents, the America of *Leave It to Beaver*, of the nice elderly couple next door and the ice cream man with his handcart, has been replaced by a country where the people feel a need to guard their children from all manner of threats and hazards.

And then they send their kids off to school. Whole classrooms of kids turn up with detailed lists of "cans" and "cannots," and teachers are asked to navigate these lists faithfully. Every year I have spent in the classroom, the files of parent forms laying out kids' needs and exclusions have grown fatter and fatter. Find a kid with a lot of purported allergies or special conditions, and the path will lead straight to an adult close to him who has a whole wardrobe of special needs too. Teachers have to pretend this is business as usual. They aren't our own kids, and we must take our duties *in loco parentis* seriously...or else.

But the situation is out of control. Over time and through great discipline, I have learned to keep a straight face while discussing with parents their kids' special issues. Some of it, though, is impressively creative stuff. One prays for the survival of the niche human, Affluent American.

For example, a couple of years ago, we set out on an outdoor education trip along the California coast with a group of ten students. We planned to do much of our own cooking and pack bag lunches for hikes and day outings. Before the trip, students and teachers together made up menus and scheduled activities, while parents filed permission slips. They were asked to tell us what special needs, if any, their children had, so we could assure that everyone stayed healthy for the week. Oh boy! The list of exclusions, intolerances, and "special needs" we were asked to accommodate overwhelmed our imaginations.

We diligently made a chart listing each student's "profile." It was a long list. No two kids shared the same needs:

- suspected allergies to peanuts, gluten, and/or food dye
- forbidden to eat nonorganic food
- forbidden to eat in any fast food restaurant
- forbidden to eat imitation maple syrup
- forbidden to drink tap water
- needs ten nutritional supplements a day
- needs vegetarian diet
- cannot eat lettuce

- cannot eat food dyes
- cannot drink orange juice made from concentrate
- must have melatonin to sleep
- must have music to sleep
- not allowed to drink for three hours before bedtime

This is in addition to fifteen different medications we had to administer among the ten kids—some required to be taken two times a day, some with food, some on an empty stomach, some thirty minutes before bedtime, some in the midafternoon.

We teachers were staggered by the demands the parents made, yet each request was sincere and described to us as urgent and essential for the student's welfare.

I've described a single trip, but this was not a one-time occurrence. Increasingly, parents see their children as fragile and unable to endure discomfort, let alone stress. They struggle to make sure there is a warm cocoon around their kids, shielding them from the big world. But it is a misdirected mission. Instead of helping our kids stay weak, we should be toughening them up for that big, bad future.

Today, we show a nature video about Africa in a sixth grade science class, one produced with little romanticizing by National Geographic. In it, there are predators chasing and downing prey and a close-up of a lion's bloody muzzle after the kill. Next day, a reprimanding call from a parent: "My daughter was traumatized by yesterday's video. You cannot show blood in class."

One wonders how this young lady will be handling puberty in a few months.

Routinely, high schools no longer have students perform real dissections in biology class. Never mind that the subjects traditionally were worms, frogs, or fish. Parent complaints have shut down this extremely effective hands-on teaching technique. Now, kids yawn and click the mouse for virtual dissections online, all the while texting their friends.

Middle school parents object to our teaching international news and keeping up with world events. They say it is too upsetting for their thirteen-year-olds. Even as they send them to the movies to see thrillers depicting cold-blooded murders.

We take students to the Sierra Nevada, staying in little cabins at the foot of Mono Pass where a pristine spring bubbles out of the hillside. The kids are afraid to drink the water, preferring to sip from plastic bottles of Dasani water—its source, municipal tap water.

A few years ago, a parent insisted on inspecting the construction records for the school building to determine whether any toxic substances might be present on the premises. When we go off on field excursions, parents will send kids with water purifiers, helmets, dust masks or bottles of hand sanitizer. Presumably, the kids still get to go to the mall and play in the park without protective gear. But maybe not.

One parent cautions us that her son is allergic to lettuce, another to carrots: distaste masquerading as a medical condition. Another parent informs us that her son is allergic to water but still wants him to come along on our sweaty five-day trip to the desert. An earnest dad explains that his daughter cannot be exposed to food that is not organic, yet she downs ramen noodles laced with MSG every day at lunch. And, curiously, no one seems to be allergic to Red Bull energy drinks or Starburst candies or Cheetos.

For class outings, inevitably some parent will write a note explaining that her student cannot sit in the back seat of a vehicle, or he will be violently ill. Many miles later, the other kids want a turn in the front seat, so we insist Billy climb in back. It never fails that he is 100 percent fine back there, if miffed. A doting mother objects to our rule banning electronics on trips. She insists her son cannot tolerate long car rides without a movie or some portable device for distraction. But he survives good naturedly, poking at and joking with other kids.

Parents send along instructions to dose their students with melatonin at bedtime. Or they explain that Suzie cannot fall asleep without music playing through her earbuds. Or the light has to stay on in the bunk room. But after a day of running around in the open air, teachers find all of them fast asleep in the dark by 10:00 p.m.

Routinely, now, parents tell us their children suffer from a sensory-overload condition and their fingernails cannot be trimmed. In the noontime tag games, though, these kids draw blood from other students' arms, so we call them indoors one at a time and blunt their talons with a nail clipper. No issue. Pretty soon, they ask to do it themselves, using our clippers at school. Or kids come to school with their long hair ratty and askew every day. The parents explain that their scalps are too sensitive to tolerate hair brushing. The parents drop the kids at school, and once they are out of sight, we hand out hairbrushes and send the disheveled students to the bathroom, explaining they can't rejoin the group until their hair is neat. They comply with no need of supervision.

Everyone, now, must have a gluten-free diet, unless someone brings in cupcakes to celebrate a birthday. Many teenagers insist they are vegetarians, but it is curious how crispy, warm bacon is an exception on every overnight trip we take. Everyone insists on food labeled organic, including chicken nuggets, but takeout pepperoni pizza and soft drinks still rule the day when kids vote for a class treat (or parents bring such foods in) for a special occasion.

The fourteen-year-old boy whose parents have written on his emergency medical form, "Fred cannot digest meat," is discovered to be consistently strong-arming other students at lunchtime to get them to turn over their roast-beef sandwiches. He devours them daily to no ill effect. Another parent applies to have her daughter admitted to the eighth grade class but only if we promise to make sure she can adhere to her Raw Food diet throughout all school activities as well as on trips.

Bernice Callahan, a mental health-care professional who taught parenting classes in the Bay Area over twenty years ago, wisely cautioned: explain to your kids that they can get away with being a picky eater or throwing tantrums in front of their parents because the love at home is unconditional; that does not translate to school or public, though. How wise she was. Today, instead of helping kids suit up for battle in the big world out there, parents try to encase them in a bubble of comfort. It won't work. And in the meantime, teachers are struggling to maintain their sanity.

8

My Kids Have Traveled Everywhere

It is true. Their kids *have* been everywhere. Parents love to talk about it. Actually brag about it. (I learned that while listening in at parents' cocktail parties.) And they are always surprised that we teachers have not taken a ten-day jaunt to Iceland, Bali, Thailand, Italy. We teach geography and history, so why aren't we traveling on our school breaks?

What's *wrong* with us?

Leading up to any school vacation period (winter break, spring break), the requests for extensions of time off come flooding in from parents. "We are taking the kids out of school for an educational trip to Belize. Please excuse Mortimer and provide make-up work for him to do, so he does not get behind. We will have him keep a journal every day on the trip about what he is learning." Nothing the teacher says will dissuade them from their plans, though the parents do reserve a measure of withering pity for anyone who does not support traveling the world for educational purposes.

So Lucy returns from her extended leave. Her trip was to Switzerland.

"What was Switzerland like, Lucy?" I ask.

"Oh, it was great. We stayed in a five-star hotel. They had room service, and they had gluten-free food. And a pool."

"But what about the country?"

"It has a lot of mountains."

"Where did you go? Do you remember?"

"Uh, I have to ask my mom. Me and my nanny got to watch Swiss TV in the room."

Scott's family went to Mexico. They pointed out it would enhance his Spanish language study.

"So, Scott, did you get to practice Spanish on your trip?" I ask.

"Sure. My dad told me one morning that we were going to take the car-o to town-o to get some gas-o."

George went to France.

"How did you do using the French you've learned, George?" I ask.

"Oh, no need. They speak English in France."

"Where did you go? What did you see?"

"Oh, it was so cool! We went to Euro Disney!"

Meanwhile, Jed's parents took extra time to travel domestically.

"Where did you go on your vacation, Jed?" I ask.

"We went to someplace close to the airport. A charter SUV picked us up."

"Was it in the United States?"

"I'm not sure. There were really good tennis courts. And an ocean."

Then there's that geography stuff too.

"Where is Europe anyway?" I ask Jeff.

"Is it kind of close to Australia? I think so, because my parents took me both places last year."

"Gail, I understand your family went to Asia over Easter break. Where were you?" I ask.

"We went to a tennis resort. I don't know the country, but it was hot. And it was on an island in some ocean."

"Ned, your dad tells me he will be away, visiting family again this week. They live in Mexico, right?" I ask.

"I think so."

"Does he speak any Spanish with you?"

"No."

"Which part of Mexico is his family home?"

"The Mexico part."

"Carl, your father grew up in Italy, right?" I ask.

"Yes, he's told me lots of stories about it!"

"Does he speak Italian?"

"Oh, yeah, on the phone all the time."

"Did he teach you any when you went there with him?"

"No."

But the argument is that travel is so educational.

We took our class on a trip along the Pacific coast to study marine life. One morning, we kayaked in a shallow bay, paddling among sea otters and seals. Tammy was visibly terrified, almost unable to paddle, even though the day was calm, and she had a skilled paddling partner. She explained tearfully that she felt comfortable only in enclosed pool waters at holiday resorts.

Given the sheltered version of travel these teenagers had experienced, we sought to offer them travel that would be expansive, broadening, stimulating.

First, we planned an excursion into the Sierra Nevada Mountains and the high desert of California. In advance of the five-day adventure, the parents made the following requests:

- "Let Jimmy bring his Gameboy in the car so that he won't get bored."
- "Call us every night to report that you are safe."
- "Don't make him eat green vegetables."
- "Don't give her Gatorade to drink in the desert—only natural electrolytes."
- "He does not eat meals at standard times but needs to snack every two hours."
- "He has to bring his own food to stick to his Raw Food diet."
- "He needs an herbal sleep remedy at night to get to sleep."
- "She needs her cell phone for security."
- "I need to hear from you every day so that I don't freak out."

On the next trip, we explain to the parents that we are going to backpack a couple of miles into a nearby state park, where we will stargaze and listen to the owls all night long. We request, "Please, make sure your students do not have any food in their packs, as it will attract varmints at night."

The parents, nevertheless, are certain their children will be deprived overnight, so they hide cookies and candy bars in the kids' packs. We are the ones who are awakened to shrieks and screams at five in the morning, when a raccoon tears apart Karla's pack to get at the sweets.

The parents are upset that the kids will have to sleep on the ground and without tents, even though we explain that the tents are too heavy for them to carry in their packs for our three-mile trek to the campsite. Marshall's mom sneaks a large bottle of calamine lotion into his pack because she is worried about the bugs out there. Marshall is struggling mightily to keep up with the group, even though he is an athletic kid. Halfway up a steep ascent, I become just too curious about why this is, and I soon discover the heavy bottle of calamine as well as a full-size bottle of shampoo in the kid's pack. So I empty both into the dirt to lighten his load.

The stories could go on and on.

The value, the essence of travel—especially for young people whose values and empathy are still forming—is to move beyond the comfort zone, to experience the world from different points of view. This means allowing oneself to taste unfamiliar flavors, shoulder a different burden for a while, step on the rocks, or put up with the rain.

Mark Twain said it best almost 150 years ago: "Travel is fatal to prejudice, bigotry, and narrow-mindedness, and many of our people need it sorely on these accounts. Broad, wholesome, charitable views of men and things cannot be acquired by vegetating in one little corner of the earth all one's lifetime."

Kids are resilient, and they are impressionable. Letting them live in the broader world for a while carries value beyond reckoning.

9

Amusing Themselves into a Stupor: The Tyranny of Having to Have Fun

Parents want their kids to be happy. Joy, pride, gratification: this is how many envision what they will experience in being a parent. And it follows that parents want their children to be happy at school, to be joyful and fulfilled by learning and growing. All of this is reasonable.

The problem is that not all learning comes easily, nor is it joyful. We have only to look at a baby trying to master the first tasks of functioning as a human to see how hard it can be to learn, how frustrating it is to master the essential fundamentals. For a toddler, learning to walk involves a lot of falls and many tears. Getting the hang of using a spoon can be so frustrating that he melts into a tantrum. And to watch an older child try to master irregular English verbs (such as lie/lay/lain or drink/drank/drunk), or try to tackle multiplication facts, or try to share a favorite toy is to confirm the suspicion that a lot of important subsequent learning likewise can be a struggle and is definitely not fun. For parents, there is a basic discrepancy between wanting a child to report she had fun today at school and wanting her to learn what she must to be an educated person. Nevertheless, in the past couple of decades, there has been a steady push for school to be more fun. And no wonder.

A teacher's major competition is the world of entertainment at everyone's fingertips around the clock.

When my students tearfully plead with me that learning something is just too hard for them, I have to remind them: if all this came to you easily, you wouldn't need to go to school. The whole point of schooling is to supervise the young as they try to crack the code and become literate, informed, and disciplined thinkers. And then there's that word *discipline*. Young people need to have their minds trained and disciplined to think clearly and logically in order to grow and be competent adults. Rarely is *discipline* described as fun.

Of course, teachers have figured out survival skills to work around this parental lobby for their kids to have fun at school. For example, open house days at school are designed specifically to highlight the excitement, color, and fun. No teacher runs a regular lesson on open house days. That would be suicide. Teachers figure out games and happy art projects or have students give entertaining presentations. More techy educational institutions, such as the new Alt School, have taken placating parents one step further: the staff send parents cheerful texts and short videos of their children being happy at school.

When parents are touring school during admissions season, I never would assign a timed writing task. Who wants to watch kids sweat over difficult work, anxiously watch the clock, and run spell check in a panic just before time is up? But they need very much to learn to work well under deadlines. We don't discuss the conflict in Syria in front of parents, but when the parents leave the room, the kids blurt out urgent questions, trying to understand why the mayhem is occurring and the role of the United States in it. It's as if, instinctually, they are drawn to the challenge of becoming competent.

In our school design, we reject the often-paralyzing notion that it needs to be fun and instead focus on honoring teenagers by teaching them the satisfaction and joy of necessary and important work. Our model differentiates between the drive for success—which can often be hijacked in the classroom by the distraction of focusing on grades or by giving students "success" at silly tasks so they feel happy—and the learning that a person acquires through facing challenges that are meaningful and hard. Dismayed at how little is asked of teenagers today in terms of relevant, meaningful endeavor, we strive to train and develop discerning thinkers, who will be able to evaluate the mountains of data that bombard all of us every day, and to inspire students to make real contributions to their community and society.

We create a culture and a school narrative that promote the essential work that teenagers need to do: define a sense of self, form values, achieve personal responsibility, and engage in difficult work. In particular, we create technology-free times and projects in which we focus intently on each other as a cooperative flesh-and-blood group. We try to help kids turn away from the uniform mediocrity of the social media feeds.

But that means we forego a lot of the bells and whistles that look like such fun, especially to the parents looking over our shoulders.

Listening and collaboration skills are central for teenagers as they mature into the adult world. But again, a conscientious teacher has to resist the activities that *look* as if they are addressing those skills but are actually just fun and games. Letting students work cooperatively on drawing a map of Europe is fine but not if the focus shifts to gluing on glitter rather than making it rigorously to scale. Having students make a video of a battle in the Revolutionary War is productive but not if a teacher sighs and lets it go when "kids will be kids" and the dates and facts are wrong. Researching an important topic is not the same as surfing the web.

It is very common for parents to complain that the work is too hard in the classroom or that we as teachers don't understand their students. Our emails and voice messages are filled with chastisements: "He is very sensitive and feels criticized" or "She is afraid of displeasing you" or "You are not accommodating her learning disability enough." Students typically climb into their parents' cars at the end of the day and dump fifteen minutes of whining: stories of inhuman stress and details of endless struggles and perceived failures from the school day.

In fact, this kind of behavior (though it creates a backlash aimed at the teachers) is healthy and productive for young people. It is beneficial to work really hard and then be able to claim sympathy from those who love and nurture them. Precisely this kind of push-pull helps adolescents develop stamina and grit, to find satisfaction in making a big effort and being acknowledged for it. The trick is for the adults to keep in mind that the dynamic is productive and necessary but not a prompt for lobbying the school to make the work less challenging.

A sage parent of a middle school girl once explained her technique for enduring this phase of adolescent strengthening. She said she would stand in front of her raging daughter and just keep saying, with heart, "Oh, really? Uh-huh, uh-huh," while steadily backing up until she could find a place to sit down and make herself smaller, below her daughter's eye level. It worked every time. The girl felt heard, validated, and justified. And then, of course, being a teenager, she would simply say something like "I gotta go" and leave the room. Task accomplished for both parent and child.

Just as weight-bearing physical exercise helps create strong bones, pushing through difficult intellectual tasks strengthens a young person's mind and overall stamina. The parent's role is to witness the struggle and to praise the hard work, confirming that the effort is worthwhile.

The key is focused effort and a belief that hard work brings results. Angela Duckworth documented the effectiveness of using this practice in education in her 2016 book, *Grit*. When a student applies effort to use his acquired skills, he will realize achievement. A simplified expression of Duckworth's thesis is "skill x effort = achievement."[9]

Nevertheless, a significant number of parents push, push, push for less work and less struggle for their students. A common rationale is that students, and especially those with learning differences, should not experience discomfort. They should be shielded from pain. We believe nothing could be further from the right course, and parents who lobby for leniency and excuse their kids because they are dyslexic, or have poor working memory, and so on, are misguided. Kids are tougher than we think. Few adults can remember the bounding energy of adolescence, and the teenage years are exactly the period during which students can train or retrain themselves to sharpen skills, improve habits, and increase endurance. Teachers have the emotional distance to do the pushing, set the bar, and require ever-increasing proficiency, but parents need to support the work. Mastering something difficult is not essentially fun, but the gratification that comes with overcoming hurdles makes having fun pale by comparison.

While maintaining a conscious focus on the struggle that authentic learning requires and holding this work as highly valuable and necessary, we have learned how critical it is to work not only on academics but also on the critical foundations of problem solving, decision making, and ethics education. The ideal tool is a group consensus practice called Council. The core of our work with young people is instilling an ability to hold fast to moral values as well as to work toward empathy for others. Much more time consuming and effort intensive than such programs as positive discipline, restorative justice, or peer-mediation techniques, Council does not elicit comments such as "this is fun!" from students. Council is hard work, and it is often painful work. Nevertheless, I have watched students again and again strap on the rigors and demands of Council because it feels authentic and just, and it's effective in unifying the group. Conflict cannot be swept away with lighthearted tactics or else it bubbles up again. We find that the significant time and energy we devote to creating consensus in Council—giving the practice precedence over everything else when conflict arises—are precisely what make teenagers value and trust it.

The Council process fosters community and trust, creating an environment for serious and focused intellectual work. It addresses teenagers' passionate interest in fairness and their yearning to have a voice in their own lives. Teaching problem solving, collaboration, and communication skills has become more valued in education over the past twenty years. Honing metacognitive skills (those specifically related to problem solving) and what are frequently termed soft skills (engaging emotional intelligence to promote communication, empathy and leadership) used to be considered subsidiary to mastering writing, math, or critical thinking. Current research and classroom experience now suggest that they are crucial for successful learning and high academic performance.

Teenagers can acquire these skills and learn to solve problems, mediate interpersonal conflicts, and dispense justice through Council. The format was developed by Jack Zimmerman and Virginia Coyle in the 1970s and described in their 1996 book, *The Way of Council*. Its use has spread over forty years and continues to be supported today by the Ojai Foundation. The system is elegantly simple, fair, and effective. Council forms the foundation of all the metacognitive and soft skills work in the classroom. Over the years, we have adapted and expanded the original model set out by Zimmerman and Coyle, sometimes using it every day to negotiate difficult times. Here's how it works.

At the beginning of the year, ideally on the first day of class, we gather all students in a group. We sit together on the floor, on the same level, so that everyone is able to see everyone else's face. The working rules are printed on cards and laid in the center of the circle for everyone to keep in view.

The rules of our Councils are simple:

- Each person speaks from the heart.
- Each person listens with the heart.
- Everyone holds a piece of the truth.

- When anyone speaks, we all listen attentively.
- We speak with spontaneity, building on what people in the circle have just said.
- Each person speaks only for himself or herself, no one else.
- Council discussions may not be continued outside the circle.

In the beginning, the teacher demonstrates how to bring an idea or question to the group so that discussion can begin. In the first Councils, we merely work to get to know each other. We ask questions: "What do you like?" and "Where do you live?" Then we move on: "What are your hopes?" and "What are your fears?" We try to focus on each other. It is important that teachers sit alongside students as equals, speak as equals, and discuss the questions as equals. We talk one at a time, in the order in which we sit in the circle. The first sessions of Council work toward establishing an atmosphere of safety, mutual goals, and collaboration.

Councils differ from class meetings of other sorts in several ways. First, we work diligently to demonstrate equality and respect for each other. No one can speak out of turn, so that helps keep all voices equal. Second, though it sounds a little silly, sitting on the floor really does change the tenor of the conversation. You might say it grounds everyone. Third, Council is a tool we can reach for at any moment, so its influence builds over time in a good way. Consensus becomes the norm.

After students understand the process, we call Council when we have a problem or need to make a decision that involves the whole group. Anyone can ask for a Council to bring an issue to the group. Someone might ask for help resolving a dispute between students or making an important decision, such as how to mete out daily chores at school or where to go for an overnight trip. Each person speaks in turn as we pass a rock around the circle.

Council inspires an extraordinary emergence of trust. Though a teacher is allowed to redirect discussion if the focus is lost or a rule is violated, everyone has an equal voice. We see teenagers and adults listen to each other thoughtfully. They pass the rock and debate the issue. There are no derogatory comments, because the next speaker will call you on it. If you speak dishonestly, someone will point this out. No one can monopolize the discussion.

I watch the light go on for each student as we reinforce the idea that every perspective is valuable. Teacher and students together are building a community in which each contributes authentically. Later, this collaboration will be carried back to academic work.

The key is that we hold Council in the context of community, a community built by sitting together on equal ground over the weeks. There is no escape from Council if you are in the community. Anyone may call a Council at any time, and we will sit. So people honor each other, knowing we will be in it together, knowing we will each be heard in turn. Each has work to do, and we fulfill our obligations in full view of each other. Everyone knows each person is making an honest effort.

Because it is the foundation for teaching metacognitive and soft skills, significant time must be devoted to Council. It is worth it to cancel class or interrupt a field trip to address a problem that is interfering with feeling safe, feeling understood, or feeling befriended.

Relationships need to stay in good repair to free students for intellectual work.

Once in my classroom, we had a Council that went on for hours. It was about derogatory comments scrawled on a wall of the school. No one was accused, because we all spoke for ourselves. A student in the circle began by saying, "I am not the kind of person who would write words like that." Another said, "I did not do it, because I am not tall enough to reach up there!" Then the discussion changed subtly as speaking from the heart kicked in:

"I can imagine writing those words if I were really upset and by myself outside."
"I can see that if I felt on the outside of the group, I could strike out like that."

Slowly, the community drew together, and the teen who had vandalized the wall realized we could all understand how he had come to do it. He felt seen and understood. With heart and compassion, the community embraced him even as it lamented his misdeed.

Eventually, after a couple of days' worth of Council sessions, the vandal admitted to the group that he had defaced the wall. Teens nodded. People thanked him for coming forward. Someone said, "I get it." The group then moved on to justice and assigned him to scrape and scrub the wall on his free time.

That was an early experience of Council for me, and I was astonished—and hooked. As a teacher, I had been ready to suspend the student. But his peers came to a superior understanding of his motivation and his frame of mind, and they also knew how to restore him to good standing in the group. The community pulled together around him instead of shunning him. It was humbling to see these young people figure out a higher justice than adults could ever manage. The group felt closer, with a stronger mutual purpose, in the aftermath. The errant teen moved back into the group and worked harder than he had before.

Council works with "mean girls" by getting to the bottom of the fear and unhappiness that provoke them to be cruel. It works with kids who claim they are bullied. I have seen a change in students who habitually miss deadlines or don't turn in work. They begin to see the value of school. Because they have found a voice, they invest. They are working on the important, nagging worries that can paralyze adolescents: "Am I liked?" or "Do I fit in?" or "Is it safe to be me?" Students subsequently can give their energy and focus to algebra, history, literature.

Once we have sat in Council a few times, the tension of unresolved problems and upset begins to dissipate. Students know they have a process to air concerns and resolve conflict. They can concentrate on learning. Though Council could be viewed as "eating up class time," every minute of focusing and attending is valuable and builds solid ground for all other endeavors.[10]

Yet, here again, we encounter resistance from parents about Council. Twenty years ago, many, if not most, of my students received ethical training in their homes. Families were more likely to be active in religious institutions and therefore there was a regular forum for young people to explore notions of right and wrong, good and evil. I see a much more secular community today and find that students come to school hungry to talk about these subjects.

At first, I was surprised at how enthusiastic my seventh grade students were to study major world religions, but they were fascinated and especially intrigued to learn that most religions share fundamental ideals of right and wrong. Council is a secular forum for these discussions, but it is not easy stuff to tackle.

Many students are confused and disoriented by the societal discourse about right and wrong. They readily point to public incidents that seem to validate just about any behavior, moral or otherwise: lying, cheating, stealing, hiding evidence, excusing reprehensible acts. In Council, we often confront members who unflinchingly lie until the embrace of the community finally convinces them to come clean. It is not unusual for a student to experience a cathartic breakthrough in Council.

For example, once a thirteen-year-old had violated a school rule about internet use; she was messaging a friend on her laptop during her lunch break. Students themselves had written a rule forbidding messaging during school hours, but this girl did it anyway. The issue was brought to Council because she denied doing it. As the rock went around the circle, other students first corroborated that they had witnessed her breaking the rule. Feeling caught, the girl began attempting to convince us she had only halfway violated the rule, or there was a loophole she had used. She would not meet anyone's eye.

The rock continued to go around the circle as other students reassured her that they understood how it had happened, that they could see how she had stumbled, that they knew how she had been tempted. They were empathetic, but the Council held firm about right and wrong. Eventually, the rock came back to the girl. She sat holding it for a long time. It was excruciating: we all had to endure two endless minutes of silence. Finally, she looked up and scanned the circle.

"You are right," she said. "I knew it was wrong, but I did it anyway. I broke the rule. I should have a consequence." It was a moving, transformative moment. She was crying, but she was smiling too.

Her neighbor took the rock from her and murmured a thank you, saying he was proud to see the girl be so brave. The next student repeated the thanks and praised her for coming clean, and so forth around the circle. We held the line on morality through the pain of it. After the Council, the feeling in the group was jubilant, warm, and cohesive. The girl continued to feel welcome in the group.

The experience, as well as those like it involving the teaching of ethics, is never fun, but it is pure gold for teenagers. Parents usually don't like to hear about this kind of thing in Council, especially the suffering. That is one important reason we hold Council work as confidential within the group. But there is very little that is more important for the development of a young person's character.

Nevertheless, parents will object. Confronted with the fact that his daughter had lied multiple times to teachers about stealing at school, one father proclaimed, "She is a good kid who made a wrong choice." He shielded her from consequences the Council wished to impose, and his teenager, therefore, was left dangling in a miserable free fall of moral opprobrium. Later, we heard the girl bragging, "I'm really good at bluffing," and we understood the deep damage that can be caused by turning away from serious work on right and wrong. The parent was so fearful of a smirch on the student's disciplinary record, or worse, mention of the incident on high school recommendations, he pressured us to overlook the misdeed, excuse her, and wipe our files clean. For his teenager, sadly, the stakes will be higher next time.

10

Not the Child I Ordered

When my first child was a newborn, my sister sent me a present. It was a recorded mix of songs. Over the years, it has proved to be more meaningful and useful than anything else to help me learn to be a parent.

Included in the mix were sweet lullabies and also funny songs about babies who would not sleep, and so on. But one song has come back to me over and over again. I would remember it as my own kids were growing up, and today I often find myself humming it unconsciously as I work with students and parents who are struggling with each other. The version of "On Children" that my sister sent was by Sweet Honey in the Rock. They set to music the words of the poet Kahlil Gibran:

> Your children are not your children.
> They are the sons and daughters of Life's longing for itself.
> They come through you but not from you,
> And though they are with you yet they belong not to you.
> You may give them your love but not your thoughts,
> For they have their own thoughts...

For parents whose children are in the final months of middle school, the words of the song are especially poignant. As parents, it is difficult and humbling to come to understand that our children are not ours. And though parents and teachers alike must shepherd children through the growing up years, we must remember that they are not the embodiment of our own dreams, nor can we expect them to fulfill our own longings.

When parents are contemplating high school choices, the issue comes into sharp focus. There is a lot of angst generated over SSAT scores and finding the "perfect fit" for a student for high school. And, too often, there is a silent anger or even grief as a parent has to come to grips with an understanding that he or she did not "get the child that was ordered," so to speak. Every fall, teachers empathize with parents who cannot accept that their child is not going to be well suited to a high-stress academic setting or a school geared toward students who are artistic prodigies. Teachers see parents become enraged when they find out the school with the manicured campus is not going to welcome every student who can pay the tuition. We see parents who consider their children as some sort of failure because they don't fit the "going to Stanford" mold.

There are so many routes that can lead to fulfillment for our children, not merely the familiar scholastic path. High school is only the beginning of the journey. The SSAT measures academic aptitude (only one kind of intelligence), not an adolescent's broader potential. It cannot predict the gifted therapist, the brilliant artist, the compassionate healer, the successful entrepreneur. Some young people putter along through high school, only to discover their genius when they hit their twenties. Some kids thrive in the big unruly mix of a public high school where it is safe and exhilarating to try on different selves. Some students know even by eighth grade that their siren call is not academics but working with their hands and brains in new and creative ways. There are infinite ways to contribute and to live a meaningful life.

As the best parents (or teachers) of our children, we may give them our love but not our thoughts...for they have their own thoughts. In fact, in listening well to our children, we as older people have much to learn. They move toward a future that we do not know and can little imagine.

Accepting our children as they are, celebrating with them as they find their own paths, is the greatest gift we as parents can give to the now-grown infants we introduced to the world so long ago.

11

Parents Who Missed Out on Careers in the Air Force

They don't even need to get licensed, they are already so good at it. Born helicopter pilots. Capable of navigating any terrain. Used to long hours. Able to lock onto the target and keep it in their sights all day long—until cocktail hour. Dedicated to surveillance.

Helicopter parents. The dears.

The head of every private middle school knows that all they care about is "target acquired." The parents use grades as their radar. Good grades assure that Johnny will have high self-esteem, and because of that, life at home will be smoother. But really, securing the perimeters (locking in the GPA) is merely preliminary in the focused campaign for the main objective: acceptance by a quality high school.

High school admissions people see the helicopter parents coming and they duck. Curiously, kids with those brilliant grades (goal secure) and good test scores often mysteriously fail to gain acceptance to the best and shiniest high schools. But admissions directors are seasoned veterans and have weathered these assaults for years. No school welcomes aerial supervision on the high school campus.

Old-fashioned strategies are out. It was once routine for parents to do their kids' homework in the evening. But now, with Wi-Fi in almost every school, parents can send in drones all day long under the radar: surreptitious texts and emailed computer files. Kids can text their parents in the middle of detention. Parents can shoot directives like missiles at the teacher 24/7 too.

Moms show up with forgotten lunch bags. Dads try to fax us math worksheets.

Nannies show up with homework, the history book, the project poster. Mom sends Grandma in with gym shoes. The clarinet. The Ritalin.

Sometimes they blow it: Mom shows up to take Tina home because she is sick. Uh, Tina is sick? The teacher has not heard that. The school nurse did not call home. Yet here the mom stands, ready to take Tina home (or quite possibly out to lunch and then to the mall).

My coteacher and I had a standard rule in our classroom: no hats. Lester strolls in wearing his new favorite beanie. We confiscate the hat and put it in the June box (to be returned at the year's end). Lester is upset, but class goes on. Within the hour, the classroom phone rings. Email messages chime. Angry parent demands a conference with teachers the next morning.

So we teachers show up to meet before school. Down the hallway stomps a dad in full regalia—perfect tan, stunning tailored suit, stylish shades, hair totally coifed at 7:30 a.m.—to confront the unreasonable teachers and reclaim the kid's favorite new beanie. I wonder why this dad is so angry and so rude. He doesn't even take off his sunglasses to talk to us. I wonder why he thinks Lester is above the rules, why we should bend our standards to his whim. We calmly maintain we will return the hat at the end of the year. Dad slams his fist on the table and storms out of the room.

How was I supposed to know he was rich and powerful and used to getting his way? The rules do not apply.

Tammy forgets to take her homework with her at 3:00 p.m. The parent leaves a message instructing teachers to leave the homework someplace outside the classroom door, so she can come pick it up after hours. We say no. This is a good lesson and will help Tammy learn to take what she needs at 3:00 p.m. Next morning, we discover that a window left ajar in the classroom has been pried open. The parent has helped Tammy wiggle in through the crack.

We saw the skid marks where the copter put down on the playground.

12

Meds and the Modern Parent

My child is just beautiful. Look at those strong legs, those pink cheeks, those white teeth! He can run and jump and splash around in the deep end of the pool for hours. He eats with such abandon, stuffing in pizza, soda, brownies, and making a huge mess in his enthusiasm. When he is tired, he just conks out on the sofa or in the armchair in front of the TV. He sleeps and sleeps—right there. For the whole night sometimes. Such health and vigor! A perfect, sound body.

But he goes to school, and they don't appreciate how healthy and perfect he is. They say he won't focus. He is messy and undisciplined. He can't keep track of things. He gets low grades on all of his papers, but I know how smart he is! He gets into fights with other kids, but he says he has good buddies at summer camp. They say his reading is weak, but he sits in front of the computer for hours and surfs—that's reading! And he reads the manual on my new phone and gets it to work.

So we went to this shrink to fix him—the same doctor the other moms use. (The teacher said his name was super familiar.) The shrink met with us, and later he met my son for a few minutes, and he gave us this prescription for...I don't know what it is, Ritalin or

Concerta or was it Zoloft? Maybe it was Prozac. One of those meds my friends' kids take. The little white ones. Anyway, he said to give it to him for school.

So in the morning, I put out a pill for him. He takes it usually, but I think he spaces out sometimes. I don't know, what with the insane rush of the morning: get up, get dressed, get the dog in the car (Darn! I forgot the teeth brushing again!), and then stop at Starbucks to get us all lattes (he prefers the frappuccino because kids like drinks a little sweet) and a pastry. There's always a line at Subway to pick up lunch, so that takes time. (Oh, he didn't comb his hair either, but that's ok, we have to wash it this week sometime.) I know there were a couple of times when I forgot the meds, but I got him a double shot in his frap to make up for it. Caffeine helps him focus, like the drugs.

The teachers tell us he yawns all morning in class and that by 1:00 p.m. he's falling out of his chair with the fidgets. Well, school lasts too long! Maybe the meds aren't right. (They should be, they're so expensive. Darn! That reminds me: I forgot to get the refill.) Well, I don't know. Maybe class is just super boring, you know? I have to call that shrink. (If I just call him instead of going in with my kid, he won't charge for another whole appointment.)

Did he eat his lunch? Only drank the soda and ate the candy bar? Said he wasn't hungry? It's those meds, you know. He tells me they kill his appetite, so we don't make him take them on weekends or on days he's going on a field trip or something. Maybe he needs more of them for the yawning? I know. We'll try giving him two in the morning for a while and see what happens. But I know for sure that by the time they wear off at 3:00 p.m., we'll be needing to stop on the way home because he'll be yelling for fries and a burger. (I don't let him eat at McDonalds or any place like that. We stay strictly organic. I don't want him eating additives.)

When they piled on the homework in the spring, we would let him take a couple in the evening to help him study. It did make it harder to sleep, but he could do homework after he watched TV from nine to ten. (That's his special treat, an hour in the evening. Although often it does get kind of late when we go out to dinner. My days are so rushed; we usually end up eating out.)

If things don't get better in a couple of weeks, maybe we should ask for a new drug. I know my girlfriend's kid did well on Adderall. Maybe we should ask to try that for a while. After all, I took some of my kid's meds for a couple of days, and they sure didn't make algebra any easier for me.

I worry about him. I do. He didn't make upper house soccer. So during the day on Saturday and Sunday, he gets bored with only video games for amusement. He's twelve now, so we let him go off on his own on weekend nights. He only has about fifty dollars in his wallet, so he can't go far. And I make him take an Uber home if it's after dark. He has nice friends, kids of my friends, in good neighborhoods. They like to have parties at someone's house. It's OK because usually an older brother is there to chaperone. Sometimes, the parties do drift out onto the bike path after dark, the one over by the mall. I tell him to be careful over there, on account of a lot of glass from smashed bottles, and sometimes there are homeless people drinking near there.

And, wow, is my son tired on weekend mornings! Sleeps until after noon! Poor kid, they work him really hard all week at school. So on

Sunday nights when he finally gets down to the homework, we have to give him an extra pill again to do the book report for Monday.

But I'm just not sure the pills are really working for him. I think we should ask the doc to switch him to something else, and then after a week or so, ask the teacher if it's going any better at school. That way, it'll be a sort of blind trial. When we finally get it figured out, it'll be great. No more homework hassles, and he'll get the grades he deserves. I'm sure the right med is out there somewhere.

MEDS IN THE MODERN SCHOOL

The love affair with medication-to-fix-anything spills over into the school, where crowd control adds to the chaos. In most schools, teachers do not administer medication to students, except during outdoor education trips. This is purportedly to keep the situation professional, with all meds in the hands of the school nurse. But given how many kids partake today, imagine the scene for the poor, beleaguered nurse! It is the noontime lunch break, and everyone is scrambling for food, kids pawing through their lockers, negotiating trades with friends, squabbling over who sits next to whom at the picnic tables.

Outside the nurse's office, a line stretches down the hallway, kids waiting to be dosed before they can eat. And they are frantic with hunger—pushy, loud, and irritable. One by one, each student approaches the nurse's desk to get meds. She has a pharmacopeia spread along her shelves, one that would be the envy of any well-heeled drug dealer, along with a binder bulging with instruction sheets for each kid. This one takes the meds before food, this other one after. A third kid needs two different meds, but one of the pills has to be cut in half, and the parents didn't do that before dropping off the bottle. Ned's prescription just changed, and the new instructions are still on a sticky note attached to his record. Suzie comes along with Grace, who is shy about getting her meds, but Suzie is an operator. She barks the dosage at the befuddled adult, who is squinting at the teensy-weensy writing on the label. Suzie hurries her to give Grace the meds so that the girls can get back to socializing in the courtyard. Kenny looks dubiously at the pills the nurse hands him and admits he doesn't think these are his. Meanwhile, another student's meds have been delivered in a little plastic baggie without any official labeling; it just says "Jakie's pills" in black marker. There are fifty squirrely kids in line to be dosed with high-power psychotropic medications—and this is only the noontime med call, not the ones for 9:00 a.m. or 2:00 p.m.

Twenty years ago, administering medication to students was a relatively rare task for teachers. In two decades, however, the number of students in private middle schools taking daily focus medication has skyrocketed until, for the past few years, most of our students were imbibing meds daily. Parents began a prescription or stopped it without telling the teachers, as if conducting their own blind experiments on the efficacy of the drugs. The situation feels out of control at this point, with adolescents as guinea pigs in experiments bereft of rigorous medical oversight.

13

Mediating the Teacher-Parent Divide

As students mature past elementary-school age, parents and teachers often begin to work at cross purposes. The strain of managing their adolescents can make parents feel as if their backs are up against a wall all the time, and the demands from teachers are firmly in the crosshairs as they look for the causes of their kids' upset, acting out, moodiness, misery—however you want to describe it. What happens, then, is that teachers are somehow framed as the enemy that parents must defeat to save their teenagers. Teachers, with experience of having watched many kids pass through this stage over the years, watch parents get in the way of the work that teenagers need to do to mature into independent, balanced individuals.

Teenagers have a deep need for adult guidance and mentoring, yet they are in a developmental phase that requires them to push away from parents in order to mature. Teachers can be placeholders for the parents in providing the needed support during these years of emerging independence. But to the extent that some teens remain too enmeshed with their parents, their development gets arrested. As this happens, often they can seem to be a sort of Rorschach inkblot test that reveals the dynamics of their families.

Walk into the teachers' lounge in any school, and you will hear endless grumbling about helicopter parents. With the mistaken aim of helping their kids, these parents metaphorically ride along in their students' backpacks every day at school. One parent put it to me boldly: "My child needs me to help her through this difficult part of her life, and I reserve the right to micromanage every aspect of her schooling." He was right that his adolescent needed adult mentoring, but when parents project their fears of failure onto their teens—who must at all costs learn to deal with setbacks and losses both large and small—they block the critical growth their teens need to achieve during middle school and high school. Trying to help parents refrain from over involvement, however, usually lands the teacher in hot water. Just as the nanny gets in trouble for winning too much affection from her preschool charges, teachers can feel like a threat to parents. Hence, the teacher-parent divide.

In all fairness to parents, their cycle of feeling fear and attempting to control is driven by the atmosphere in middle and high schools today: focus on GPAs and test results, and the perceived need for kids to be involved in a dizzying round of extracurricular activities. It is a highly competitive race that kids are thrown into: they must get into the best high schools, to be admitted to the best colleges, to land the best jobs.

This can lead to crazy behaviors. In the past several years, I have noticed it has become routine for parents to lie for their students. Parents have looked me in the eye and said, "Tommy is sick in bed and can't come to school," but Tommy was at a baseball game last night until 11:30 p.m., and he is staying home to sleep it off. Parents call in to say their student needs a "mental health day" but curiously enough, there is an important math test scheduled for

10:00 a.m. Parents will say that the internet went down, so Suzie could not do her homework, but Suzie's best friend lets it slip that she went out to dinner last night and got home really late. A parent of one of my students once helped her son break into school after hours to get contraband that had been confiscated by the teachers. Parents write papers for kids. They swear their kid is not playing video games on weeknights, though their son cannot help bragging at school about his fun time late Tuesday night with the newest game. And on and on.

From a distance, any parent would see that these actions are not productive for the healthy growth of a teenager, but they find themselves in such a bind and are so mistrustful of teachers and the system they represent, that they do this stuff anyway. And then have to lie.

A second level of ill-conceived strategies finds parents seeking medication to improve their adolescents' behavior and focus. Statistics have revealed a broad uptick in teens' consumption of psychotropic drugs over the past decade, and my own observations in the classroom reveal a shocking acceleration in this practice. Over the past ten years, it has become routine for adolescent boys to be on one of several "focus" meds: Concerta, Adderall, Ritalin. Often, parents try to hide this from teachers, but any educator seasoned in the classroom picks up on the cues very fast.

Frequently, parents will start or stop medications without telling the teacher—"just to see if there is a difference." Of course, in the classroom, the teacher witnesses a pronounced change in the student and reacts to it. There will be drama about the student's sudden shift in behavior: acting rowdy, missed work, or squabbles with classmates. One parent, unusually forthright, arrived late one morning with her student and apologized: "I'm sorry, I forgot to give him his Ritalin. I just bought him a double espresso at Starbucks to make up for it. He should be fine." And the teacher thinks: Right, only ricocheting off the walls for the whole morning and driving everyone nuts.

Parents get pushed into letting their kids double up on the meds for test prep nights. One of my students was desperate to be admitted to a private high school, and confessed to me, "My mom let me take a second pill last night so I could really focus, but then I couldn't get to sleep." Or parents will allow their students to stop taking their prescriptions when the kid lobby gets too intense. In their harried lives, most parents don't take their kids to the psychiatrist for the expensive periodic check-ins but just monkey with the med doses themselves to try to optimize performance.

In the current environment in middle schools and high schools, it is an endless cycle of competition and attempts to game the system. Using meds may seem a reasonable, if an ill-considered, remedy.

EMAIL AS THE MAGIC WEAPON

In short, parents demand from schools more comfort and fewer challenges so that they can find some relief from the stress and upset that their students bring home. Their ultimate tool is email, the battleground where the teacher-parent divide really heats up.

I, too, once had the role of being the parent of two children in a private school. How I managed to survive those years of angst and upset without a magic sword is a puzzle to me now. While others were battling it out against teachers and triumphing in cyberspace, like an idiot I was awkwardly standing hat in hand at the door of the classroom, asking whether I could maybe have a date for a parent conference. But it is so easy to ask for something you may not deserve or lash out at someone in a moment of pain when there is a nice computer screen as a shield. You have to be truly stupid not to use the magic weapon.

First, back in the 1990s, it was the Blackberry. In those first heydays of instant communication, it was very cool to be the entrepreneur with a Blackberry clipped to your belt. About one month into fall of one year, Donna turned up in the classroom, offering me my very own Blackberry, as a gift. She had sent nine messages that day and was frustrated that I was not answering her (but instead teaching her kid). I glanced at that bulky chunk at her waist and instantly decided it was not an accessory I could incorporate into my look, so I politely declined the gift. Best fashion choice I ever made. Donna, who was trained as a financier, wanted to offer commentary, criticism, and advice on educating her student around the clock—even on vacation—and I was turning down access to an invaluable resource: her agenda. She stayed miffed for months.

Then came Y2K, and we all got wired: a computer in every kitchen and one on every teacher's desk. Gone was the telephone message machine, along with its helpful little delete button. Now all day long, the email was jamming up with messages silently hunkering in the void: "I think maybe Jimmy will be sick today," and "I didn't give Eliot his meds this morning," and "Oh, we found lice on Jenny last night, but I forgot to tell you." These messages came from parents who had driven their kids to school that morning, but didn't get out of their cars, balancing the latte, you know. We would be off on a class field trip for the day. Every parent had signed and sent in a permission slip for the trip, but still, there it was in an email at 11:00 in the morning: "I will be picking Sarah up at one o'clock to go to the orthodontist." At the end of the day, the teacher catches holy hell for having taken the kid to the art museum.

Ah, but email as a weapon of the darkness gives a parent such satisfying power. Late at night, after prolonged battles with a teenager over homework and the messy bedroom, it is a relief to pour a drink and then reach for the laptop. There in the stillness of midnight, all of the censors asleep, parents can really rip into the teacher.

After a couple of years in the email trenches, I learned to look at the date stamp of every message (especially the two-page ones) before reading (or deleting before reading). The 1:00 a.m. whoppers are all the same, and I quote: "You are unfair, you are unfit to teach, you are a sadist, you should have your license yanked, you are assassinating my child's character"—blah, blah, blah (with lots of grammar errors). This unfailingly occurs following an F on a final or an incomplete on a long-term project. But! Next day, the midnight warrior does not even recall the battle he waged in the wee hours. He will come into the classroom after school, joke around, talk football, and make no reference whatsoever to the issue that drew blood in the night. "Man, aren't kids a piece of work? I don't know how you do it." He doesn't notice the bloody bandages around the teacher's head either.

The email superheroes of all, though, are the private school parents who decide they are switching schools and simply send an email to announce dropping out. They will get "better value" elsewhere. There's no offer of a chat to explain, no personal phone call. No handshake, no moment for the student to say good-bye to everyone. There's no pretense of honoring the year-long enrollment contract with its financial obligations. Simply an email informing departure. It's like canceling garbage pick-up during vacation, really. That simple. Email can make all those messy human interactions unnecessary. So easily can you erase the long-term relationship with the person who cared for your child for a year or two. This is the same person (teacher) who held your kid's head while he puked on the class overnight trip. Who tutored your kid during her lunch period. This is the person who got your kid to give a speech in front of a crowd for the first time, write an essay, hold a reptile. An email is sanitary, easy. No sloppy emotions or push back from the other side. Type, send. Done. Moving on.

If you pay the private school to teach the child, it's really like paying the utility company to give you electricity, right? From your smartphone you can negotiate both relationships with equal ease. And teach your kid to do the same with the people in his or her own life.

THE "C'MON, SWEETIE, LET'S..." STYLE OF PARENTING

It is a phenomenon of baby-boomer parents, those raised in the regulated, disciplinary 1950s to 1970s, before the top blew off self-control and traditional values. The parents are very smart, well read, earnest about raising their children. They have tried Montessori programs, green schools, single-sex education, and "last child in the woods" programs. At least the mothers have.

The kids are largely boys—extremely intelligent, quirky, intense, energetic boys. They have been this way since birth. They are highly verbal and know what they want. The mothers are smart, loving, and they don't understand they're playing in the major leagues with these young goliaths. Most often, the fathers are onlooker dads or very stern dads (absent, working hard to make money, or confused by parenting). The burden falls on the poor mother: and she's been madly in love with this child since his birth!

The boys trumpet staggering proficiency in a couple of areas—often math, but sometimes the talent is reading-based, and the kid has a prodigious vocabulary, though some of it's a bit off, as if, maybe, he's never been corrected. The boys know what they want, and they want it now. They are loud. They are demanding. The mothers are trying to be even tempered, trying not to raise their voices, trying to give their sons independence and selfhood and full rein to develop their outsized brainpower. The mothers are trying so hard and worrying a lot. As educators, we feel for them. But they're doing their kids such a disservice. We call it the "C'mon, Sweetie, Let's..." style of parenting.

The boys elbow into a new environment, all bravado, whiz-bang math skills, and fifty-cent words flying off the tongue. They interrupt. They can't sit still. They do what they want, when they want. They don't understand commands or comments like, "Wait," or "It's someone else's turn to shine," or "Maybe some of what you think you know you don't actually know."

Many years ago, a child psychiatrist I know took on a four-year-old boy who fell into this category. The therapist confidently told the parents, "It will take three sessions or so, and then we will see some change in your son." Well, it took more than six years. After five sessions, the psychiatrist had already summed it up: "Your kid plays hardball, so you better learn to play it too, for his sake."

The parents of kids like these need to eat their Wheaties to hold their own against the strong, willful intelligence that their kids are offering. The truth is that these kids are running wild with a scary kind of freedom: Why do anything when "let's" is a part of the equation, and no consequences force compliance? These kids are very smart, and at a terrifyingly young age they've learned to game the system, to their own detriment.

Everyone tiptoes around these self-centered young geniuses. Given that, it's no wonder so many are described as having nonverbal learning difficulties. No one has been willing to take them on since they formulated their first words, which one could readily imagine were, "Do it for me, and do it for me *now!*" They never needed to read nonverbal cues because no one ever dared establish an agenda that didn't mesh with their own. But then, and now, they need strong, consistent, intelligent training to understand this is a world in which all of us have standing and that no one is 100 percent right.

Kids like this need boundaries. Teachers face a vertical climb when parents continue to use "C'mon, Sweetie, Let's..." at home, while in the real world these kids do need to sit down and be quiet, let other kids talk, wash their hands, consider someone else's contribution, clean up their messes. Parents who are afraid of setting the tough limits that are essential to building self-control and self-reliance are damaging the children they love so dearly. But the good news? It's never too late to begin anew.

THE CRISIS OF FAITH IN THE SPRING OF EIGHTH GRADE

There is a sort of crisis-of-faith moment in the spring of eighth grade, just a few months short of high school—always. Adolescents cling desperately to their old ways in hopes that life as they knew it in childhood and elementary school can be resurrected. There is huge resistance to being fully engaged in study or to moving a big academic project to fruition. Students seem suddenly to have abandoned exercising self-control and muscle and judgment, and they increasingly indulge in self-denial in terms of time management.

Every year, some eighth grade student (often a boy) has to take the hard road of not finishing a big project in late winter and then having to give up spring break. Some of these students—the fortunate ones, the ones whose parents jump in with strong guidance and firm limits—see the light after that and make wholesale changes in the way they see their "work" for school. They then begin to embrace their lives and who and what they are about, for the long term. They become intellectual explorers, not merely soldiers begrudgingly doing what the generals tell them to do.

This is what we hope for in education. We hope we are creating lifelong learners—inquisitive future adults who will make the world a better place. We hope they won't simply feel they've been "sprung" from school and slump into lethargy. We hope they will grab life and make something big of it. We hope they will learn the great joy of hard work done well.

14

Placing Community-Building Skills at the Center

In my teaching over the past fifteen years, as I began to prioritize teaching metacognitive and soft skills, I saw students grow more focused and efficient across the curriculum. Developing emotional intelligence provides students a grounding inside themselves from which they can launch into hard work that will demand stamina, self-confidence, and perseverance. Starting an academic year by focusing on metacognitive and soft skills, the nuts and bolts of community-building skills, gives students a running start on success. In this way, teachers offer students a solid base as a springboard to go far.

A scaffold of strategies, in addition to the central work of Council, is essential in establishing community-building at the heart of the classroom. The guiding principle is timing. While many schools incorporate classes in these skills into a weekly class schedule, I have found that working with a student precisely in the moment of dysfunction is key: it shifts the lesson from the abstract to the concrete. And giving priority to teaching these skills as the need presents itself serves to give status to the work and emphasizes the value of emotional intelligence and collaboration.

Spontaneous lessons catch students in moments of heightened receptiveness. Anyone can call on his or her "better angels" in role play or after the fact in a moment of reflection. When students are taught something such as problem-solving skills in regular lessons at predictable times in the weekly schedule, they tend to respond in a disingenuous way, bored by the proceedings. It is easy to glibly talk about how you should act, but it's hard to follow through in a moment of crisis. It is in the urgency of the moment of conflict that students can appreciate the power of becoming a good communicator, and they will work much harder to learn.

FIRST: CREATING THE SKILLS ATMOSPHERE

Early on, the teacher must establish an atmosphere of safety, trust, and common purpose for students at school. Almost thirty years ago, David Heath, the founding head of Marin Primary and Middle School in Larkspur, California, and a great leader in education in the San Francisco Bay Area, impressed upon his faculty that there are three essentials for any child to thrive and learn at school: (1) she must feel safe, (2) she must feel she is understood, and (3) she must feel she has a friend. Relationships are primary. This is community. It takes work to create and maintain community, but the investment reduces social isolation and bullying, and it frees students to make a focused commitment to academic work.

Similarly, the framework for teaching both metacognitive and soft skills in the classroom has three parts: (1) students must be certain they are known and safe in the group, (2) we must work on group interdependence (the talents of each individual are put to use), and (3) we must work on community and trust. After the framework is in place, we can move on to problem solving, conflict resolution, and collaboration. In our school, we discovered that this framework can be built efficiently through teacher-led small-group excursions off campus, through larger group overnight "unplugged" trips far from home, and through group problem-solving in Council. No budget, special equipment, or infrastructure is required. The strategy can work in any school.

SMALL GROUP CHALLENGES AND ADVENTURES: STUDENTS FEEL KNOWN AND SAFE

The first part of the framework achieves the buy-in for superior academic effort and commitment by reassuring the student that he or she is known and safe. Small group excursions are an effective tool. Early in the school year, students are organized into small groups, close friends separated into different groups when possible. The value of gathering a limited number of students into an ad hoc smaller group is key: connecting to others face to face and eye to eye is powerful. A group can be as small as four students, but a group of no more than twelve students is ideal. (Organizations such as Outward Bound, Esalen, and the Experiment in International Living discovered this optimal number years ago.) Each student needs a chance to interact with everyone else, to see and be seen by everyone. People struggle to do that in groups larger than about a dozen individuals.

Starting the year with small-group challenges sets the stage for everything. It breaks the ice, loosens everyone up, and sends a message that we are going to be working together in ways that feel very real in the moment. We set out first in small groups as a signal that we are all paying close attention to each other.

Once students are divided into different groups, I (and perhaps a coteacher as well) take one team of students at a time on a day-long outdoor adventure somewhere off campus. We find a destination that is new to every student. It can be in a state park, an urban open space, the campus of a local college, or the shores of a lake or ocean. We may climb a rugged trail, bushwhack up a streambed, explore an abandoned section of an old graveyard, find a huge oak tree to scale, or scramble along the coastline at low tide, exploring from one beach to the next. I choose an outing that seems a little out of bounds, a little daring, something that demands we all work cooperatively to make the day successful and safe for everyone. The more unusual and unfrequented the location, or the more bizarre the challenge, the better. We establish an atmosphere of cooperative play for the day.

The group is students and teacher on their own together, and it has to be small enough for everyone to "be" with one another. This also diminishes the teacher's advantage—the power ratio is diluted, so to speak. The teacher is doing exactly what the students are doing. Everyone is equal clawing his or her way through brush or climbing up and over boulders at the surf line. Students see the teacher struggling, sweating, mustering the energy to overcome a challenge, and needing help over a rough spot. The teacher sees students in a new light: who is agile, who is timid, who lends a hand, who charges ahead. Often, these traits are hidden amid the books and keyboards in the classroom. There is enormous value in appreciating each other in our full human dimensions.

The challenge of the day does not have to be extreme. It simply needs to demand that everyone helps everyone else. The same work can be achieved by exercises such as ropes courses, but the beauty of an unanticipated, unstructured adventure cannot be underestimated. The task for the day is amorphous, demands ingenuity and cooperation, and inevitably will create some sense of togetherness.

Later, back at our desks, we have shared stories that make us laugh, and we remember that we all face the same struggle in working toward goals. As a teacher, I can coax a better effort from a student who is frustrated with a writing project by asking her to take on the attitude she used climbing in the canyon. I can remind a student who is too nervous to give his speech that he was the first one to jump off the boulder into the water. And they can believe me when I tell them I struggle to master difficult material just as they do.

If we teach our students that meeting new challenges is a lifelong practice, not one merely for kids, they are more likely to embrace this idea as empowering and fulfilling. Daylong adventures together, helping each other, and cooperating go a long way toward modeling that.

GROUP OVERNIGHT TRIPS: STUDENTS LEARN TO VALUE INTERDEPENDENCE

The second part of the framework is established through large-group overnight trips. These build on the skills and trust first created in the small group outings. Ideally, we go into the wilderness, but if that is not practical, a destination new to everyone will work. The whole class lives with each other for a couple of days, roughing it a bit, cooking, housekeeping, and bedding down in sleeping bags. The goal is to live and work as a self-contained group for three to five days, without outside contact of any sort—no TV, no computer screens, no ear buds, no phones. The trip needs to be longer than a single night to give the group time to coalesce as a social unit and to let go of the outside world.

The results are heartening and beautiful. Students discover new friends and appreciate their classmates in many ways. This even begins if there is a long drive or hike to our destination. Face to face over a few days, a group gets to know each other well. Students and teachers see one another stumbling around sleepily in pajamas in the morning and struggling to peel potatoes for dinner. We are present to and for each other all day long, watching each other adapt or flex, hit highs and lows. Over a few days, the "other" becomes "me." Community is reinforced. Cooperation becomes the default. Empathy grows.

This sets the stage for real work on problem solving and collaboration and on people skills. A 2014 study coauthored by Yalda Uhls and Patricia Greenfield of the Children's Digital Media Center at Los Angeles corroborates my experience of the value of group trips. Uhls and Greenfield described a UCLA experiment with a group of sixth graders. They spent a week in a mountain camp setting with no access to screens. The results: compared with the control group, which stayed home and played with electronics, the camp group showed measurable growth in the ability to read emotion in other people. The researchers noted that the lack of screens, along with the focused group interactions over several days, contributed to this growth.[11]

The absence of electronics on a trip far from home keeps us sharing and attending in the moment. Without one hundred Instagram friends, students turn to the real friends at their sides. Everyone is on equal footing: a classmate's social status depends on how kind he is, how much he is willing to smile, and how well he pitches in to cook dinner or wash dishes. No glazed eyes and absentmindedness.

The wilderness is a superior destination, but finding an isolated location closer to home can work when wilderness travel is not feasible. A group overnight could even be held on school grounds, ideally in a part of the school that students don't usually frequent. Again, it is important for the group to be self-sustaining in food preparation and housekeeping, free from electronics and outside communication. Students with disabilities can participate in group overnights to the extent that their physical ability to be independent allows, and this greatly increases empathy and tolerance in the group as everyone helps each other and lives together for a few days.

The stories that emerge from overnight trips establish a strong narrative for the school culture. They cycle back through conversations for months, even years.

THE COUNCIL PROCESS: TRUST AND COMMUNITY

Experiencing intimate small group adventures, students begin to feel they are known, they are safe. Later, on large-group overnight trips, we build beyond this to interdependence. New friendships emerge and community is built. Finally, when we sit in Council, students are primed to develop empathy, improve their communication skills, and take turns at leadership as they solve problems and make decisions together by consensus. Council is central to maintaining community.

The three-part framework we developed over the years in our school established a strong and resilient core of community, freeing our students to focus on academic goals. Placing community-building in the center taught me that if students hold themselves outside the group or above the wisdom of their fellows, then there can be no fairness, no collaboration, no resolution. Consequently, upset and fear interfere with classroom work every day. But there are very few teens I have known who would not agree to sit on equal ground and be seen, in a Council setting, if given the chance. Teenagers care deeply about justice and fairness, and to achieve this they need the safety of a community with tenets that support listening and collaborating. Building that kind of togetherness takes time. Before academics and sports, before social life and extracurricular activities, community building that culminates in Council can set the stage for success.

As students and teachers sit in our community's Council circle, we see around us a microcosm of the larger world that we must learn to understand and negotiate in order to thrive.

15

How to Tame a Teenager: Life-Altering Adventures in the Outback

Our school's annual trip to the empty, scorching desert of California demonstrates very clearly how travel can help us empower adolescents to be everything they can be, to have stamina and grit.

I love taking young people on their first trip to the desert. For years, we have hauled groups of young teenagers to the Mojave Desert. Yes, those snarly, surly, noisy, self-indulgent louts who are impossible to live with. The same. Every single trip is memorable—beautiful, scary, too hot, too cold, breathtaking, uncomfortable, hard, thrilling. We leave home with a group of coddled, whining brats and return a week later with young people who have begun to feel their own power and selfhood. It's exhausting work, and it's worth every effort.

Why is it that the wilderness is a perfect venue for moving young people toward independence, compassion, and fellow feeling? It seems to happen on every trip. No one emerges from a desert trip untouched. Maybe it's because nothing is there, and we make something of it. It's empty except for what we learn to find there.

We embark on desert trips whose destinations are remote and itineraries largely open ended. We don't have a plan except to arrive in the Mojave. At first, kids hate this idea. Where are we going to sleep? What are we going to do? When will we get there? What time are we eating, going to bed, waking up? It's unnerving to leave our lives behind. As the schedule evaporates and the miles unwind, there is nothing but ourselves, the land, the couple of moving vehicles that hold our compact lifeline: food, water, shelter.

And soon, everyone begins to sense the liberation inherent in this state. What we usually worry about in our daily lives—this is trivial stuff. Out in the wild, the worries are essential and real. Do we have fuel? Do we have water and food, plus extra for emergencies? Do we have tools for repairs if a vehicle breaks down? This is thrilling. At no other moment in our lives does our planning matter so much. Vigilance and care take on an urgency that makes us feel alive.

It feels very real: break the rules out here, and you can end up dead.

Teenagers love this kind of thing! We are harnessing these rebels and giving them a cause.

On the first day of the trip, we have to drive a long, long way. From the San Francisco Bay Area, the Mojave Desert is at least a ten-hour drive, if not longer. We drive open jeeps on the trips and bring along a truck or van that has air conditioning. Yes, it's crazy to drive ten hours under the broiling sun in an open jeep, but this is the initiation phase. This is how you get "out there." Among the adult drivers, in fact, taking turns in the truck or van with the AC is a duty, not a privilege. The point is to immerse in the place: the foggy coast, the scorching interior farmlands, the pine-scented climb over

Tehachapi Pass. After ten hours on the hot, windy road, adults and kids are on equal footing.

The first night, we camp in a primitive area on purpose, to be fully out there. We find open ground on Bureau of Land Management (BLM) lands, or in the far reaches of a national preserve or park, and we circle the vehicles amid the sage.

"This is it?" some kid asks. This is it. He does a 360 and surveys what he can see. The conclusion: nothing. Right? Wrong. No one comes here—that's why we are here.

The first encounter is always fun to observe. Stunned disbelief.

We drove all this way to get *here*? There's nothing but rocks and stunted plants. It's 7:00 p.m. and still over one hundred degrees, and a cracking wind is kicking up. There's no place to sit. There's no water faucet. The toilet is a smelly, spider-infested outhouse. It's hotter and more extreme and more awful than can be imagined.

"My parents would hate this," mumbles Carter.

Hey! My parents would hate this! This is the first epiphany, and worth a lot.

We poke around in the dirt and scrub while we wait for the charcoal to burn down to coals. The little rocks underfoot are so many different shades of red and pink and white and mauve. Approaching a sage plant provokes frantic scurrying of three whip-fast lizards. A hawk sails overhead on the thermals. The sky turns coral and turquoise as the sun begins to set. A star. An almost-silent rockslide up on the hillside. Tiny yellow buds on a cactus. What a world where there seemed to be nothing!

Then, dinnertime. In fact, it is way past dinnertime. It is 9:00 p.m., and no one has served food yet. On our trips, it is up to the kids to do it all. They have a job chart, and they have been trained back at school, but it wasn't dirty and windy back there. And in addition, they weren't this hungry back there!

We are someplace none of us has ever been before. We are out in the unknown. Who knew the wind would kick up like this? Who knew the steaks would still be frozen solid in the cooler? That the chip bag would split and spill all over the ground? That someone would kick sand into the guacamole? The only way to make it through is to figure it out: there is no "right way," and there is power in having to make it all up, but make it up right so that things work out ok. This, too, is secretly thrilling. It is important work: we're all really hungry. We can't go buy more guacamole. There's no microwave. The challenge lights everyone on fire, and they wake up, start creating. It's a sight to behold, as the adults sit back and admire. Don't ask us for the answers; you have to figure them out, or we won't eat tonight.

The first day is fairly miserable. The learning curve is steep. Kids will try whining and pouting because that has always worked with their parents. We time it on every trip. First, Eddie set the record: a prolonged pout lasting six hours. (He was in the back seat of a jeep, though, so no one could hear him complaining because of the wind and road noise.) Next, it was Jessie. He pouted for a day and a half because it was hot. Slowly, he figured out that he was getting more and more thirsty and hungry while everyone else was managing to get along: they were covering up in the sun and constantly sipping liquids. They were eating what we had. So the cookies had fallen into the dirt, so the Gatorade flavors weren't the best, so the bread was getting pretty dried out. Finally, Jessie put his hat on and sat in a spot of shade, nursing liquids and eating nuts to get over his heat stress. Fairly soon he managed a smile or two.

The desert is empty, and you fill it as you will. It's rougher and more extreme than anything in the world. There is no plan. There's no destination. No clocks, no itinerary, no requirements beyond survival. Everything that students do, every move they make, counts. Their decisions carry huge consequences. They are making it up. They are making a life. This is what it is to begin to matter in the adult world.

Students are willing to put up with a lot of discomfort and chaos on road trips if they're running them. One year, our students decided we should travel to the Sierra in winter and stay in a Sierra Club wilderness lodge. It was a do-it-yourself place, and in January, temperatures hovered below freezing with daily snowfall. As it turned out, the lodge was in terrible disrepair, but we did not discover this until we had moved in. The woodstove didn't draw, and we coughed in a constant smoky haze. The kitchen was a veritable ptomaine palace, inches deep in months and years of communal living grime. The roof leaked, and it was almost as cold indoors as outdoors. We could barely see our humble macaroni and cheese in the dim light of too-few lanterns. But our students loved the trip! They figured out solutions as best they could, reveled in their independence, and embraced the squalor precisely because it was their very own. The adults complained more than the teenagers, but the kids had chosen the trip, and they owned it. They even ate their own lousy cooking with just a shrug.

Teachers witness pronounced personal growth on trips, but they also witness it in the classroom. It's rewarding to see how fast and how much students grow when they feel ownership of the process. It takes a lot of faith and, perhaps, some well-placed commentary or doubtful remarks by the adults, but teenagers can and will figure out how to learn and mature and become competent.

16

Why I Wear Stain-Resistant Clothes to School

Teenagers are experts at nesting and housekeeping. It's just that their habitats are unrecognizable to adults as civilized dwellings. Look at the gewgaws they assemble on every surface, the piles of reeking apparel they amass on the floor, the ketchup-smeared, sugar-rimmed, crust-laden dishes stacked up in towers beside the bed. They are domesticated, to the meager extent that their skills and lack of training allow.

Teenagers are adept at personal grooming too. Even the most disheveled thirteen-year-old boy devotes time and care to a hidden vanity point: a haircut, a pair of brand-name basketball shoes, a logo-emblazoned sweatshirt. The adolescent girl who balks at washing her hair owns clusters of bottles and sprays and finger pots of beauty products. It's just that there's a line drawn between hygiene and self-adornment.

But adults call them slobs. Teenagers and tidiness: How can you even write the two words in the same sentence? Messy, smelly, sloppy, lazy do-nothings. Teenagers resist hygiene or tidying-up routines; they run up dental bills for cavities; they see no connection between zits and lack of soap; they don't notice dust balls or overflowing garbage cans.

Parents rant about trying to get their teenagers to embrace clean-liness and tidiness. It's an unending struggle of outmaneuvering each other, employing threats (adults), or using delay tactics (kids) until a crisis is imminent—the kid will be late for school, or the parent can no longer stand the filth in the bathroom or the dog poop in the backyard. A job chart for each day (designating Saturday morning for a routine of chores) and work completion tied to allowance will inevitably fail at home. It is demoralizing—infuriating is more like it.

But we never hear parents talk about on-the-job training. They seem to have abandoned that odious but critical task. Teachers take it on. Kids step out of the Lexus or the Land Rover, and we get to work introducing them to foreign objects, such as soap, brooms, wash-cloths, plastic garbage bags.

The students are chatty and matter of fact about what goes on at home:

> Lisa tells me, "My mom yells at me to clean up my room, but I know she'll get tired after a while and forget that she threatened to ground me."
> Kim tosses off this one: "Oh, my sister and I don't make our beds or anything. That's for our nanny to do. We do school."
> Kristy admits, "I only wash my hair when my mom makes me do it, but she spaces out."
> Max comments drily, "My parents don't like me to mess with our dishwasher. The cleaners do all that."
> Rusty points out, "If I leave my dirty clothes on the floor long enough, Mom picks them up and washes them."
> Bonnie crows, "We have Hispanic people who do that."

Yikes. So many kids arrive at their twelfth birthdays devoid of life skills and clumsy at seemingly simple tasks. Among my recent students, Jim could not figure out how to operate a broom. He just flicked crumbs and dust into the corners. Jenny got all tangled up trying to make a bed. Cleaning a toilet repelled and disgusted all of them. Terry complained we needed to buy a new vacuum for the classroom because he had never heard of emptying the filled-up vacuum bag. Jeff and Lisa tossed dishes into the drying rack by the sink, so they all crashed to the floor. When teachers demonstrated how to mop the floor, the students considered it the wildest fun they had ever imagined. Many adolescent boys cannot tie shoelaces, button a coat efficiently, fold a t-shirt, pack a backpack, place papers in a neat stack. I have met only two kids in twenty years who were skilled at cutting up a serving of meat on a dinner plate.

Again, the kids are little tell-alls:

Jed explained his dad buys him Velcro shoes so he can get them on faster without bothering to learn to tie laces.
Kelly explained that she and her sister always eat dinner with the nanny because their parents go out a lot.
Kat was taught to throw out a pair of pants if it gets a hole in the knee.
Cal confesses that when his family eats in a restaurant, his parents put the kids at a different table, so they can ignore the noise and the mess.

In the power-struggle atmosphere of the typical home, kids rarely get any training in housekeeping and personal hygiene skills. Adult patience and dedication seem in short supply for teaching these boring but essential skills. It's easier and more appealing to farm it out—to school.

Virtually every parent of the kids I have taught has found reincarnation as a "foodie" of some sort: five-star restaurants, Asian fusion cooking, avoiding genetically modified foods. You name it, they've tried it. But somewhere in the evolutionary process, the kids all got left behind in caveman times. Their approach to eating is Neanderthal style—maybe worse, since lots of Neanderthals, after all, did live in France at the dawn of French cuisine.

They serve themselves bacon or pancakes from the common platter with a lunge and a grab, mostly without benefit of silverware. Fingers are backhoes. Lips are noisy suction devices. The fork is operated like a snow shovel, the knife like a spear. Spoons are for full-tongue licking, held vertically. They eat peanut butter out of the jar using an index finger and sip hot chocolate like a cat, with their tongues. Drinks are clutched with a vice grip while food is scooped into the mouth with the other hand. Napkins carpet the floor. Kids chew with their mouths open to the max, as if accommodating at the very least a woolly mammoth leg bone. The net effect of the caveman eating style is the helicoptering of food in a three-foot radius from a kid's chair. Then he steps on it and squishes it into the carpet when he catapults from the table to grab a fistful of cookies for dessert.

At the start of the school year, before teachers dare take students to eat anywhere in public, we have to teach elementary table manners. Teachers shriek, "Fork to mouth, not head to trough!" Chunks of food tumble out of their mouths, drinks are slurped. Spaghetti gets sucked up, lips to the plate, red sauce slapping left and right.

Hands swipe mouths and noses, then shirts and pants. A teacher with a weak stomach will never make it through the school year.

Yet my students brag about eating out at pricey restaurants and staying in fancy hotels. They are poetic in describing yellowfin sushi and Baked Alaska. No bottled salad dressing, please! No hamburger that is not grass fed. They are authorities on how to season a filet mignon. The parents find it amusing and a little quaint that we try to teach table manners. They had never considered it necessary, really. These little darlings have been taught to spend money but not how to be civilized.

17

Secrets of the Teenage Housekeeper

What an impossible concept—a teenage housekeeper! Teenagers are allergic to housekeeping.

Except they aren't.

On the first day of school, our tactic is to introduce the notion that we all share our space, and that it belongs to everyone. We make decisions together about how we will use the kitchen, the bathrooms, the common rooms, the students' study carrels. As a group, we come up with rules we think will work. We all stand on equal footing as we decide this stuff. The kids care deeply about where their study carrels are located, and not often is it because they want to be near a best friend. They just want to be the deciders.

We get the rules down fairly smoothly, except for the kitchen. The kitchen is perennially our biggest source of conflict. As it turns out, teenagers, like all of us, can agree quite amiably about rules for housekeeping in most places: flush the toilet, mop up spilled water, make sure trash lands inside the can, keep hands off other people's belongings, wipe your feet when you come in the door, separate the recycling. When we have a sly violation of these rules, we can usually come up with simple solutions fast, and everyone agrees.

Ah, but not about the kitchen! We began year one of our school with a rule: clean your own dishes after you use them. But you know how it goes: you cook up a hot dog, then someone wants to use the pan after you, and probably that person will want the ketchup and mustard you got out, and maybe want that half a bun you left on the counter. So "clean up your own" had to be quickly abandoned (after several heated discussions), and we instituted daily kitchen jobs on the job chart: wash dishes and clean counters and microwave, with a third hand to help out.

This system disintegrated too. "Wash" was interpreted variously to mean scrape and wash, or wash and allow food bits to clog the drain, or wash but never dry until all the dishes we owned were piled in a top-heavy tower by the sink. The third hand tended merely to kibbutz. More discussions. And more. But there is the revelation: the teenagers asked for us to sit down and discuss the problem, and they led the conversation in figuring out solutions. They were absolutely passionate about using their own kitchen. They had firm ideas and clearly defined styles about how cleaning and tidying up were to be done. They attacked the outrage of filth and squalor like the most obsessive 1950s homemaker. It was fascinating.

And they had patience to revisit the problem again and again. We hauled out the crusty and greenish offal from deep in the bowels of the refrigerator and displayed it in our Council circle for everyone to claim his or her own mess fairly. The kids got down on their knees to figure out whose sauce was slimed along the kitchen baseboards. They chipped food out of the microwave to see whose lunch had exploded.

Once we held a meeting for over two hours trying to ascertain (could anyone recall?) which person had discarded a half-eaten turkey-and-cranberry sandwich on the kitchen table and left it there for two days. They cared deeply about all the details and were willing to give up recess to solve the problem and make nice the source of all their food.

Kids developed pet specialties too. Max fell in love with the dishwasher, wistfully reporting that at home only the "cleaners" were allowed to operate the dishwasher, and it was thrilling to be in charge of ours at school. Elias adored mopping the floor for the same reason. Jason developed a passion for scrubbing, and once he discovered bleach, he became lethal in his quest for sanitation. Even when he came back to visit after graduation, he pushed students aside after lunch and took over cleaning up the kitchen. On the last day of school, Lee and Emma cheerfully commandeered the refrigerator, emptied it completely, scrubbed it down, and dried it to a gleam. Other kids attacked the big old iron stove and wore out several steel wool pads scouring it.

Meanwhile, in the bathrooms, other students used up an entire roll of paper towels and a whole bottle of cleaning fluid to disinfect the sink, toilet, floor, stall doors, windows, and doorknobs. (OK, so their socks were bleached orange. We got several angry emails from moms later that night.)

If we let the kids use the hose, they would wash the teachers' cars every day of the week. They adored spraying the white boards with that smelly cleaner and restoring them to pristine snowiness. They loved the vacuum, especially after they taped a "Mammals Suck" bumper sticker on the side of it. Back and forth they would go, creating a bedlam of noise, one kid on either end of the school. And when they came to us to announce, "The vacuum is busted. We need a new one," they were thrilled to learn how to disassemble it and dislodge all the wads of paper and wrapped-up hair that were clogging the works. One kid spent many recess periods figuring out how to reassemble a vacuum we had completely torn apart, totally mesmerized.

What's going on? Teenagers in love with housecleaning? Pride in possession? Procrastinating before math class? No, it's the meaningful work. How often do we allow our overgrown babies to contribute in ways that are so palpably and obviously beneficial and satisfying? They definitely need to be trained—a lot, over and over again—but washing dishes or vacuuming or disinfecting keyboards are jobs that they can begin and complete in an enormously satisfactory way, to the appreciation and admiration of the entire community. They feel worthy and useful. They can contribute and feel important. These tasks, in the teenagers' own space, are acts of love, really: feathering the nest, feeling worthwhile, making a difference that counts.

It is very hard to get them to do this at home, of course. But teenagers are eager to learn this adult proficiency, as long as it is on their own terms. But their own terms don't mean a level of filth no adult could stand. It just means they own the process, and they get to determine the protocols. At school, we have to change the job chart all the time. They point out that doing recycling and trash is too much for one person, so we need to split the job. Disinfecting is easy, so add dusting shelves to that job. Teenagers love to move a push broom down the hall with a load of dirt collecting in front of it. They adore any job that requires a squirt bottle. Give them the whole roll of paper towels, and they will clean the entire kitchen floor if you want.

When the tasks are even harder and require some ingenuity, you can get an even better buy-in from teenagers if they see the tasks are critical for keeping their community solid. The first time we camped with a big group of teens on national forest lands, we followed standard primitive camping protocols and instructed each of them to dig a six-inch cat hole for personal waste. Abysmal disaster. What we created was a minefield of poorly buried waste that we had to painstakingly backfill before we could leave our campsite.

Later, we adopted a group strategy. At school, before our trip to camp on desert lands, we held a training session about the group bathroom. To a roomful of nervous giggles and blushes, I demonstrated how to unpack and set up one of those toilet chairs for the elderly—the gangly gray monstrosities that are meant to straddle a regular toilet but provide trusty handholds and four-legged stability. Dandy for use over a hand-dug latrine pit, I reasoned. Everyone learned how to set up the toilet chair, and we explained there would be a two-foot-deep pit under it. A shovel (meant for digging out a vehicle stuck in a rut on a fire road) would sit by the latrine to use for backfilling after each use.

The demo ended. Pause. Of course, first we have to figure out who will dig the latrine pit...

Every boy in the room was straining forward with his hand waving madly in my face: Me! Me! Me! Digging the latrine with a dangerous-looking pickax was a spectacularly popular job on every backcountry trip we took from then on. No matter that the diggers also needed to be the backfillers and latrine seat cleaners at the end of our camping, the boys were deliriously thrilled to be in charge of the latrine. Men's work. Takes muscle. Makes it all nice for everyone. We are the strong male providers.

Universally, the group was enthusiastic about hauling dead wood out of the forest for the fire. Likewise, dragging big rocks into a circle for a cooking pit. Pumping water from the stream through a hand purifier for endless hours? We had a ready line of volunteers. Packing the pickup truck with the duffels and securing the load with bungees: everyone wanted to help.

Children crave meaningful work. They can see right through "make work" foolishness. They want to be valuable, needed, essential, just as adults do. They want to contribute. We rob our teenagers of that fulfillment by denying them essential work that makes a difference to the group. Teenagers want to do the housework in their world. We just have to let them own it.

18

Morality, Teenagers, and Limit Setting

He was my best student in English class but was unsure of himself. He worked hard; he really wanted those As. Now it was the day of the final exam. He dived right in, typing furiously on his laptop, head bent. I roved among the students. Every time I came toward his desk, he squirmed in his seat, changed the angle of the computer screen. My teacher radar went off.

I kept circling the classroom, peering over shoulders. Until I knew for sure.

After the exam, when everyone else had left, I explained what I had clearly seen him doing: toggling to his stored notes. I ripped up the printout of his exam. It was a terrible moment for both of us. But I was the adult. I owed him the truth of right and wrong.

I sat beside my student, feeling miserable too, but remembering that teaching right and wrong is the central work of all adults, and especially teachers. We are training the next generation to do the right thing.

After he finished sobbing, my student looked at me teary-eyed and blurted, "Thank you."

For stopping him—now.

Years later, he still stays in touch.

As a teacher, I see the difficult terrain teenagers negotiate as they establish a sense of self, assembling personal values and ethics. Parents may not have the stamina to teach the really painful lessons, and the digital world where teens live today is an echo chamber of immaterial relationships. Cause-effect and acts-consequences are obscured if not hidden. There are no referees. Meanwhile, teens watch others take shortcuts to get ahead, to grab success. So they, too, do something wrong because they saw other kids do it and "nothing happened." Or they think,

> No one will find out.
> Everyone does it.
> My parents do it.
> No one will get hurt.

It is critical to talk face to face to teens about ethics and to defeat the idea that a bad act can be "technically" OK. "Technically" provides the ultimate escape in any difficult discussion of truth and falsehood, right and wrong. There are so few sobering examples that can really impress teens: dead or alive, pregnant or not pregnant, HIV positive or not.

Excruciatingly aware of what goes on in their group, teenagers have little subtlety of perception. They do something wrong because it seems that other kids got away with it. No one discovers that the school denied a diploma to the senior who plagiarized. Parents will fight disciplinary action when their student "tells just a little lie."

But adults dare not be polite in teaching right and wrong. Moral values crumble at a terrible price to all of us.

It is critical for adolescents to have firm limits during their teen years, precisely because the main thrust of their maturing at this stage is to explore the breadth of their capabilities, as well as their limitations. The role of all adults is to maintain the firm boundaries of responsibility, acceptability, decency, and productivity in the face of teenagers' efforts to test those limits.

This can be confusing terrain for adults to navigate, and especially for parents. To some extent, each parent is still back at that first moment of awe, when he or she held the child for the first time. Imagine that cradling gesture, the parent's head bowed in mute adoration, gazing into the baby's eyes. Humans are hardwired to protect our young with ferocity, and unless a parent experiences a great deal of emotional or other trauma, the protective reflex toward one's child survives for years. In fact, the "mother bear stance" tends to persist even past the moment when it begins to interfere with an adolescent's necessary developmental work—pulling away to establish independence and a separate sense of self.

The design of our school explicitly addressed this issue. As teachers, we sought to coach and encourage parents to step back, to allow their teens to stumble into their own selfhood, painful as it is to watch the messiness, the drama, and the endless back-and-forth. Teachers recognize that almost all parents will have to go through a lengthy and stressful process: pulling away, getting pulled back in, reasserting distance, stepping in again to rescue their teen, getting angry and withdrawing, feeling remorse and approaching once more. This process is the normal course of things for families with teenagers. Through various aspects of our school model, we maintain systems and practices to help parents negotiate this transitional time. We heartily embrace the old adage, "Mistakes are opportunities to learn." We expect teenage students to struggle, because we know it will make them stronger, more confident adults.

An effective way for any adult to approach setting limits for teenagers is to chant slowly, "Testing, testing, one-two-three-four...testing." When adolescents are being their most beastly—swearing, ranting, slamming doors, and so on—this mantra is a lifesaver. They are testing the boundaries of their world: what is safe, what are their responsibilities to family and others, what is decent and moral, and, yes, what is legal. Healthy teenagers will test the limits in every arena. A gifted therapist and mother of a teenage girl once told me that every day she practiced understanding this by looking at herself in the mirror and repeating, "Today my daughter will reject me, and that is a sign of her health."

However, in today's world, the scenario at school is often different.

Parents scold us and say that it is too rigid and too dogmatic for teachers to hold the line and enforce right and wrong with their adolescents. "Kids will be kids," they insist. "Throw the book at the other kid, but mine is a good kid who just made a bad choice." Or "The rules were unclear. Teachers were sending mixed messages." Or "The other kid did it first and didn't get caught, so my kid should get off the hook."

Nevertheless, I am haunted by what I have seen—the real un-pleasantness, even tragedy, when those kids grow up to be dis-honest adults who casually flout the law and cheat. I have seen the teenagers I once knew as stumbling seventh graders get sent to prison, attempt suicide, lose themselves in homelessness and despair, descend into addiction. Obviously, there are complex reasons. But I suspect that the difficulty does not originate with the kids.

Morality is a lesson that calls to young people. They all begin as idealists and romantics. They want to believe in fairness and truth. They are willing to be knights in the battle for right.

Parents are often terrified their children will not succeed. They themselves have been kicked around by life, and at all costs, they want to save their children from the same. It is understandable but regrettable. Where there is fear of failure, ethics take second place.

In the big picture, the competitive atmosphere in education and especially in private schools has led to an antagonistic atmosphere, in which parents feel that their best interests and those of their students are in direct opposition to the interests or agendas of teachers and administration. There can be little other explanation for the pervasive cynical attitude that leads parents to tell an innocent, trusting young person that the system is so fundamentally rigged that cheating is the only option.

The unspoken rule seems to be, "Do what you can to get ahead—just don't get caught. And if you do get caught, lie."

At school, though, kids seem incapable of keeping confidential the advice they get from home. Inevitably, teachers hear what parents have advised, and there is the dilemma for teachers.

HOW MORALITY PLAYS OUT AT SCHOOL: VERSIONS OF REPEATING PATTERNS

—We are on our way to the Palace of Fine Arts one fine Thursday, when from the back seat, a student informs me she will help out at the entrance kiosk by "doing what my dad always tells me to do: stoop down so I look like a little kid to the lady at the ticket window. I can get in for half price."

—A dad offers the classroom a bootlegged word processing program so the school can avoid buying it. He explains they do that at the office all the time.

—A girl confesses that her mom is short on cash. She juggles the family budget by putting off paying school tuition month after month because the school doesn't charge the standard business finance charge rate. So that's money saved, but the daughter is troubled.

—The parents stay mum and also coach their student simply to pretend all is well at school until after the exciting (and, to the school, expensive) weeklong outdoor education trip. Only then do they quietly execute the plan that has been prepared for weeks: to pull the kid out of the school, skip on the remaining tuition due, and go to the new school that has already accepted their student weeks ago.

—A student's parents ask for a parent-teacher conference in early January, just before high school applications are due. We discuss their daughter's less-than-stellar GPA. The parents casually offer me a pricey gift certificate. Is this a token of appreciation, or an exchange for a little "sprucing up" of the semester report card?

—After school one day, a nervous student shares the burden she has been carrying: her dad tripped over the cat in the night and broke his arm last week. But since it happened only two days before a big storm caused the electrical lines to come down and hit their house, he is claiming the injury on the electric company's insurance claim form and saving a pile of money. She is worried and not really sure if this is the right thing to do.

—The parents sign the permission slip verifying that their daughter is "water safe" for the school's wilderness adventure trip. They don't want her to miss the excitement! Carefully, they caution her not to reveal she can't actually swim, and later this student nearly drowns as the class is crossing a swift-moving river on a hike.

—It is an everyday occurrence when the parents (or the nanny) complete homework, term papers, flash cards—you name it—but tell their student to lie that he did the work himself. The teacher can spot these ruses quickly, because the homework assignments are glaringly superior in quality to any work the teen does in class. But now the teacher stands between kid and parent on the knife-edge of cheating.

—Students are genuinely outraged when they earn zero credit for the paper that contained plagiarized text. Not a gentlemanly C, but an F. Parents threaten the school with legal action.

What adults can and must do is work to maintain the long-held values that cement flesh-and-blood relationships. A school classroom provides solid ground for this work. We need to help teenagers understand the far more tenacious endurance of the reputations they create in the day to day with real people, in real time, with real consequences, both good and bad. How will each be known? As the one who cheats, the one who steals when no one is looking, the one who tells white lies when it is convenient, the one who takes the biggest slice of the cake?

Morality cannot be taught in the absence of a flesh-and-blood group. The nature of asynchronous communication and the baffle of avatars online make it too easy to abdicate, to disappear. In my experience, students respond earnestly and deeply to the work we do face to face, when we grapple with personal responsibility, ethics, integrity, and honesty.

Central to teaching morality is explicitly revealing the consequences of acts. Many schools today deal with disciplinary issues in the privacy of the administrative offices. An infraction is treated as a private error that is not the business of the general public. This is the opposite of what should be happening and the opposite of how we have learned to deal with discipline in our school. Students and teachers talk explicitly about mistakes. We discuss consequences, and we accept that stumbling is a necessary part of learning to be an ethical and responsible member of society.

Teens need to be exposed to the real-life consequences of their acts. Otherwise, moral standards are just so many words floating unsubstantiated in the air while business as usual continues. No one knows that the exam was torn up because the student cheated: it is a private matter. No one knows the promiscuous boy or girl is now HIV positive. No one knows that a high school acceptance has been rescinded because in late May, a student broke a rule and lied to teachers about it. We are consumed, it seems, with privacy in one arena while we display ourselves naked in public view on the internet. It is a curious contradiction. Discipline by the social group is often meted out online in a very public and explicit way, but in daily life with real human beings, we hide behind the fiction of preserving an adolescent's privacy.

Yet on campus today and with greater and greater frequency, the teacher who explains and defends morality is cast as a clueless chump who doesn't get how the world works. This teacher is viewed as someone who is getting in the way of a young person's success. Parent is pitted against teacher in a race where all that matters is who comes out on top.

In rare moments of frankness, adults will admit that there are some nasty things they have done. In truth, we are not proud of these things. We protested when a company enforced its contract. Our faces got red when the officer stopped us for rolling through a stop sign. The self-talk was "white lies," "That big corporation won't miss this money," and "That law is stupid." We managed to get ourselves ahead, or not, but we have to admit privately that these were moments of personal failure.

But we have a second chance with the next generation: we can teach them better and inspire them to do the right thing. Why would we do otherwise?

19

Meaningful Hard Work, Rewarding Challenges

It took several years to convince my long-time teaching partner to undertake the big task of starting a new type of school for young teenagers. However, in the atmosphere and culture of the private school where we had been working, the quality of our teaching was deteriorating. Class size kept increasing and bureaucracy intensifying. We were hamstrung trying to respond swiftly and effectively to our students' needs or to keep our teaching high caliber and inspiring. We felt that small and simple would be better.

Our new model reaffirmed the principles we believed inspire and energize teenagers in the best ways: putting personal relationships first, assuring each student that he or she is well known and appreciated, making our curriculum relevant for our individual students, and honoring students by never "dumbing down" the content as if they were less than capable of learning. If we can "catch" adolescents in this final window of accelerated intellectual growth and guide them firmly and with good attention, we stand to help them become deeper thinkers, more principled citizens, more compassionate individuals. Time and energy lavished on teenagers as they stand at the cusp of adulthood is an important and worthy commitment of resources.

We designed our school for a group of about twelve to fifteen students (maximum) with two teachers. (A third teacher assisted part time.) We wanted to work with kids spontaneously, to ask a great deal of them, and to give them in return a great deal of our own attention and energy. For almost all human beings, the personal touch is powerful and inspiring. Remembering the teachers who had made an impact on our own younger selves, we designed a model that reasserted the value of a community in close conversation about knowledge and learning.

Going against the tide of our times, our model rejects the idea that computer apps can be substitutes for real teaching. We do not see that adolescents respond authentically and wholeheartedly to computer screens or that they stand to develop fully mature intellectual potential without dialogue. We believe in the art of teaching, human to human.

Some might object that not every teacher is up for this kind of immersion, because we have to be "on" for the entire day (or for days in a string, on trips!) with no break. But it feels authentic and essential: there are no "planning periods" in real life, and there are no schedules for when real people have urgent needs. Human beings are wired for connection with each other, and the less attenuated that connection, the more powerful. We have found that the returns for in-person attention and commitment are enormous. The guiding principle of our school model is pushing the envelope of what it is possible for young people to achieve—in every arena of their lives. A teacher who knows the student and is witness to achievements is the necessary catalyst.

TEENAGERS BOUNCE

It is enormously rewarding to work with adolescents because they are so energetic, so resilient, so willing, and because they *bounce*.

The apathy of the late teenage years has not yet set in, and the stumbling fragility of pre-adolescence is behind them. Adolescents from about twelve to fifteen are charging ahead on a path, whatever path it is, and are beautifully open to being challenged, pushed, and mentored. Even if we, the teachers, make mistakes, every day presents a clean slate to try again.

Kids this age *believe,* for better or for worse. It is not by chance that cultures around the world seize this moment for ceremonies of initiation into adulthood. Young teenagers are passionate up and down the full range of the scale every hour, every day. It is enough to drive any parent insane, but it is an inspiration for a teacher. They'll try...anything! How about extreme hiking? Extemporaneous public speaking? Conducting the school day in Spanish? Learning to operate a car jack? Reassembling the skeleton of desiccated road kill? Climbing an 800-foot sand dune in 107-degree weather?

There are challenges to working with teenagers. The main issues are related to authenticity, fairness, excellence, compassion, and a strict demand for clear thinking. We have seen the techniques we use transform adolescents. It is valuable and essential work.

A DESIGN BASED ON RESEARCH

We designed our program to be responsive to the fundamental characteristics of adolescents' brain development, providing training and experiences that promote healthy growth for teenagers. Brain research in the late 1970s began revealing how our brains are shaped by experience and environment. In *The Teenage Brain*, a recent book by Frances E. Jensen, the author explains the basics of what research has shown about adolescents: "There is a logical reason why [brain] plasticity is front-loaded in childhood and adolescence: survival depends on knowledge of one's environment, so the young brain must be flexible and moldable depending on the type of environment in which the person is growing up."[12]

Our model provides a consistent environment that encourages deep understanding, cooperation, tolerance, authentic discussion, empathy, and nonviolent conflict resolution among students. We value broad, deep, relevant learning coupled with constant self-reflection and forthright discussion in Council.

Students work hard and play hard, but they sign on for this willingly. They sense it as a point of entree to the adult world. We talk openly from the first moment of class about the lack of intellectual rigor that broadly describes public discourse in our country today. Students are intrigued that they can gain mastery of tough concepts and complicated issues and then expose falsehoods and misinformation that pervade our daily lives. They seize the opportunity to be able to locate the sites of incidents in Iraq or Syria, to understand the chemistry behind the toxic algae bloom that cancelled the California crab harvest in 2016, to understand the latest Supreme Court decisions. Becoming well informed begins to feel revolutionary! Other educators, such as Rob Riordan, cofounder of High Tech High, a network of California charter schools, have discovered this too. Teenagers, who are focused on their two main imperatives, resistance to authority and valuing contributions to community, are truly "rebels without a cause." They are longing for a way to possess agency, to make things happen, to make a difference.[13] If we suggest to them the notion that rigorous, deep thinking is subversive or that toiling along a remote trail is an extreme adventure their parents would not like them to do, they respond with enthusiasm and energy. As Sebastian Junger puts it, "Humans don't mind hardship, in fact they thrive on it; what they mind is not feeling necessary."[14]

We believe stress can be beneficial in stimulating growth and acquiring mastery, be it intellectual or physical. Our model relentlessly promotes "gritty" behaviors: do three drafts of every essay, present the required weekly speech without notes, increase mileage on the daily PE run every week, memorize one hundred bones in the human body. We hike in the rain and in the summer desert. We haul three hundred pounds of trash off a local beach in one morning. Students write a thank you note to every visitor or volunteer who comes to campus. It is good to sweat! There is no such thing as "I don't know how." Instead, we focus on, "I am learning to do this."

The perception that any one of these endeavors is edgy or excessive actually tends to cast it in a more appealing light for teenagers. It becomes a satisfyingly rebellious act to tough it out, to attack big obstacles, to go against the flow of usual, safe (boring) behaviors.

The day to day at school centers on the practice of Council, which serves to moderate all activities and couch challenges in terms that are productive for intellectual and emotional growth. Discussions and decision making, the meat of Council, specifically target the work that teenagers' emerging frontal lobes are learning to undertake: understanding of others and their different points of view (insight), deciding wrong from right (judgment), foreseeing long-term outcomes of decisions and actions (abstraction), and breaking down difficult tasks into incremental steps that will promote success (planning).

We capitalize on teens' brain plasticity to implant healthy strategies, skills, mind-sets, and values that will smooth the rough ride through adolescence and into adulthood. We offer students big challenges that they (and especially their parents) initially consider insurmountable. As they overcome hurdles, they become believers in the power of perseverance. The time we spend imbuing students with good practices and strong skills is richly rewarded later on. We are training young brains to work optimally later in life. This foundation is critical.

What all of this looks like in practice: campus visitors tell us our classrooms feel and function differently than those in typical schools. Our school trips are even more unusual in terms of the independence and agency we hand to the students. These practices pay off.

DAILY LIFE ON CAMPUS

We start the day much later than most middle schools, acknowledging what research has revealed about the circadian rhythms of adolescents. Class starts at 9:00 a.m. First, we have a brief discussion of the top international news stories of the day. What did students hear on NPR radio on the way to school? Did discussions at the United Nations yesterday bring any results? Did the Senate pass the bill for funding? Did the latest statistics on the US median income and poverty show progress or deterioration? We look at the map and plot Mosul, the Spratly Islands, Nairobi, the Philippines. Students are handed copies of critical news articles from the *New York Times* to read and study.

We ask students to consider why the media carry certain stories and how the stories are relevant to their own lives. There is no excuse to act as they see so many adults acting—to shrug and act stupid about

US foreign policy or the difficulties Congress is suffering. We consider why we should be informed about events in Afghanistan or the fate of trade talks. Students are encouraged to be well enough informed to challenge the powers that be. We remind them how little time they have before they will be voting, paying taxes, possibly even joining the military. The news becomes essential. Teenagers are excited to be in on the discussion of adult matters and to be asked for their opinions. They will work hard to contribute if given a voice.

Next, everyone runs a mile, or more. We devote about twenty minutes to vigorous physical exercise to start the day, pumping up respiration and heartbeats, clearing out the cobwebs from sleep. This practice was inspired by research described and analyzed by John J. Ratey, MD, in his 2008 book, *Spark: The Revolutionary New Science of Exercise and the Brain*. The author reviews studies beginning in the 1990s among US middle school and high school students showing that vigorous exercise enhances brain function, pronouncedly so in the hour or so following the workout.[15] We follow the *Spark* strategy: each student runs in the morning. The goal is to exercise to an individual heart-rate target, pushing for a personal best each day regardless of how fast the run actually turns out to be. The point is to get a short, stimulating workout. What we witness is a group of groggy teens stumbling out the door in the morning chill but returning a quarter hour later energized, lively, and ready to get to work. Ratey documented how physical fitness is critical to academic achievement. We have seen the success with our own students.

Students then fill their water bottles and disperse to different classrooms to get to work: an hour of math calculations or an hour of reading and discussion in history. California state curriculum mandates studying world history from CE 500–1789 in grade seven, for example, which we do. But our approach differs from other schools in that the teacher does not determine the whole curriculum. The class will have decided in Council which topics to explore in greater depth. So, for example, one year we may dive deeply into the history of Vietnam, including America's stakes in that region of the world. As we look at any period in history, we also pay special attention to news from that region as it unfolds every day. Studying ancient China enlightens us about territorial struggles among China, Japan, and the Philippines in the East China Sea. US history includes studying current cases being heard in the Supreme Court of the United States.

We conduct classes seminar style. Often, the schedule of classes changes to accommodate the need for a longer block of time for, say, a science lab or to listen to a guest speaker. Issues such as wasting time in class, being disruptive, or not completing work are brought to Council, and students themselves devise solutions. When they make the rules and policies, they follow them with care. The "us versus them" dynamic of teachers versus students is dismantled.

In addition, each student has a block of time every day for silent, independent work. Once students realize that this independent work period will lighten their homework load in the evening, they use it productively and quietly. It usually takes several Councils in the beginning of the year to drive home this point, but with time devoted to convincing students and winning them over to good time management, they happily embrace it. They will even decide in Council to arrange their study carrels strategically distant from close buddies so that they are not tempted to talk or goof off.

RELEVANT EDUCATION

In designing a better school model for adolescent education, we selected a name that is an acronym: REAL, or Relevant Education and the Art of Learning. Relevancy is key.

Our goal is to teach students to think for themselves, to embrace problem solving, to be "can do" types of individuals. We strive to instill in them a driving lust for learning, for understanding the world, and for being open to many different kinds of intellectual exploration. We work to help them understand how to discriminate between precise thinking and reasoning and their opposites. We teach them to identify bias and to figure out its bases. We urge them, as the saying goes, "Don't believe everything you think."

This is not easy stuff, and it is not a linear process. Nor does this kind of teaching bear much resemblance to prepping for standardized testing. Though there is a place for testing in the acquisition of intellectual competency, it is neither the ultimate nor the only measure of understanding. Our students do learn to study for and take tests. We work with them on strategies for mastering complicated material, memorizing formulas for verb conjugations, and getting a grip on dates and events that shape a meaningful perspective of history.

Nevertheless, our greater emphasis is on creating in our students the skills and mind-sets that promote comprehension of information they will encounter on their own, over time, for the rest of their lives. Ultimately, learning to write is the discipline of learning to think clearly about a subject, whether a student is writing to demonstrate mastery of established ideas or writing to set forth new and creative concepts. Our curriculum is writing intensive, not SSAT-prep intensive. We follow the teachable moment and adapt class content to the responses we receive from students in the day to day. We place a strong emphasis on learning in the field, learning "by the seat of one's pants," learning by reaching higher than they think is possible and pulling themselves through. And we teach through play.

None of our students will tell you that our program is all fun and games. Students readily report that they work harder than they ever imagined possible. But they will also tell you that they play harder, with more abandon and with more freedom than they ever have before.

We know we designed a pioneering program in rejecting "teaching to the test." We honestly do not believe that every child is cut from the same cloth and bound for the same future. We struggle against a one-size-fits-all approach to education and also against the notion that education is a race. To see a student learn to love reading, volunteer to get up at dawn to look at a planet through a telescope, give up recess to dissect a shark, or spend an entire Saturday at a speech tournament—this is our measure of having achieved relevancy in what we teach. We hope to send into the world young people who can look at problems and discover new solutions, find fulfillment beyond the dictates of popular culture, and be true to their inner selves.

This is relevant education as well as the art of learning. There should be more of it for our teenagers in schools.

WHAT GRADES SHOULD MEAN

Student evaluation—grading—is in many ways the most miserable aspect of teaching. We as teachers are called to the art because of the joy and transport of seeing the intellectual light ignite in a young mind. For a dedicated teacher, there is a trajectory of fulfillment like none other in watching a student burrow in, grapple intensely, and discover sudden comprehension of a difficult concept. The development of mind brings delight that is shared and amplified, teacher to student and back again. The excitement of ideas, the thrill of exploration—that's our goal in the classroom.

Inevitably, education requires periodic assessment, so we find ourselves doling out As, Bs, Cs, and Ds, effectively transforming the delight into what some see as an economic transaction. Well-trained consumers that they are, students and parents alike often regard grades as a commodity for which they can bargain and wheel and deal.

We look at grades as an indicator of a student's level of mastery of a subject, not as a reward or prize. We schedule tests and other assessments at logical intervals in the delivery of the curriculum to check to see the degree to which a student is grasping ideas and internalizing understanding. An A student has the curriculum content firmly in hand: he or she can think at a higher level about the material, can form original ideas, and can apply knowledge in other arenas. B students are approaching mastery but are not quite able to manipulate their understanding with confidence. C students are beginning to understand and have some ideas under control but are far from competent across the board. And so on. We grade students with full consciousness of each one's learning style or challenges. Grades are indicators of how independent a student has become with the subject matter. Grades are not bones thrown to compliant dogs. And, no, grades are not torture devices rigged up at inconvenient moments to catch students off guard!

And yet, though assessment is a logical step in figuring out how well a student is learning a subject, parents and students ask us almost every day to negotiate the grades. *Ask* is the polite word for *manipulate*.

"May I take the easier version of the test?"
"Can I get credit, even though I did not spell the key terms correctly?"

"Will you write a good recommendation for me, even though I pay little attention in class and rarely turn in my work on time?"

"Can I take the test with my text or notes open [because I don't really know the material, but I want that glittery A]?"

But we are striving to provide authentic feedback so that students do know the truth about how well they are learning and how well they can function on their own after they move on in education.

The mantra each semester when we hand over report cards to our students is, "Please, don't ask, what did I get? Instead, ask yourselves, what kind of evaluation did I earn?" Our grades are meant to give a clue to students about how well they are learning and how close they are to reaching full potential. A grade of B means, "We know you could master this subject more fully." We don't give our students "pity As," as we know they can always grow stronger and climb higher.

The practices we set in place every day on campus carry over to enhance the success of the times we spend on trips as a school.

EDUCATION IS NOT A RACE
Sometime over the past twenty years, education became a relentless race. Especially among upper-middle-class parents, a vogue has developed for having one's very bright preschooler shunted ahead of his peers to enter school before the official start date. It has become a mark of distinction: "My child's so bright, he's surely a prodigy. He must surge forward!"

I'll say it very clearly: what a mistake that is 99 percent of the time. At the middle school level, we see the dismal outcome of such ill-conceived efforts to rush one's child forward toward "success."

The best analogy I can come up with for the process of educating kids, albeit a clumsy one, is the old-fashioned three-legged race. Two people strap themselves together, one person's right leg tied to the other's left. Then, at the starting gun, the ungainly couple races down a field and toward a goal post as impromptu Siamese twins. The progress is lurching, unpredictable, sometimes hilarious as various human parts flail. They progress unevenly yet steadily toward the goal.

And so is the process of educating a young person. There are moments of soaring, but they are accompanied by moments of crawling. We cannot predict which skills will develop and to what extent, as others languish for months on end. Unbeknownst to his doting, starstruck parents, the four-year-old who can read at the third-grade level has not mastered the art of sharing the ball on the playground and will be shunned by his playmates. The five-year-old who has memorized the states of the union will not be able to write out legible ABCs and needs time to figure out how to share his knowledge. The math prodigy will lack a social conscience. The extremely verbal girl will be unable to grasp a number line. And on and on.

Human beings need many skill sets to function fully. The narrow window of competence covered by an academic regimen is just that—very narrow, limited, and restricted. When we hurry children along by observing their academic strengths, we are blinded to the full range of what they need for growing straight and true. We need to keep the well roundedness of the individual in full view.

The root of the word *education* means "to draw out, to bring up." Any fool knows that racing from one place to the next means we will miss details along the way. Why are we in such a hurry to have our children get through school and be spewed out into the world? Why not let them grow up, show their strengths when they feel ready, and flower in due time?

Our model encourages parents to consider giving their students the gift of a "gap" year. The practice for older students of taking a year off between high school and college is very effectively applied to some adolescents. The middle school gap year takes place either between the seventh and eighth grades or between the eighth and ninth. Gap students get an extra year to allow developmental growth to catch up with intellectual strength. Especially for those who arrived at middle school with the proud badge of having skipped a grade early on, an extra year to consolidate social learning is particularly invaluable. There is no more miserable sight than an intellectually precocious eleven-year-old trying to socialize with kids a year older—kids who are a year more steeped in hormones and, usually, not at all compassionate to those who are less mature.

Nature cannot be hurried along. Education is not a race.

ADOLESCENTS ARE STRONGER THAN WE CAN IMAGINE

Adolescents possess a measure of stamina and energy that is hard for adults to imagine. While well-heeled parents in suburbia raise a chorus of concern or outrage about too much homework, sports schedules that are too demanding, the harried pace of speech tournaments, long-term research papers or biology tests, our kids are merrily squandering hours and hours of unsupervised time trolling the internet, playing computer games, gabbing or texting on cell phones, and indulging in an activity deliciously described as "hanging" with each other. Hanging they are. Our adolescents do not have enough to do that is meaningful and purposeful, so they fill up their resumes with pursuits of their own invention—something, anything—to soak up all that excess energy and drive.

In past generations, young adults aged twelve or thirteen found themselves thrust into meaningful, productive work in the adult world. They were ready for it, as are our kids today. It is worth noting yet again that this is the age designated in almost all cultures for the ancient religious rituals conferring adulthood. We, instead, shackle our children in a prison where they can find no real, valuable contribution. To do work that engages and expands, that challenges and rewards, is one of the greatest pleasures of human existence. Yet we tie the hands of our young people, bind their bursting energy, and consign them to an extended childhood in which they have little chance to make something of their world.

As I worked with my adolescent students over the past months, I heard much dismay from parents about the workload and the multiple demands I as a teacher placed on their kids. They were working on an eight-week history research project while simultaneously training for an important speech tournament. In addition, they were asked to continue with the usual classwork: daily math, daily reading in social studies and science, daily memorization of new vocabulary and structures in Spanish. They needed to set aside time each day to read a book of their choice for a half hour for pleasure. Yes, there was struggle. Yes, a few had tantrums and gave up for a time. Some got Fs for not doing homework. Overall, however, the sense of joyful purpose that pervaded the school was beautiful to behold. We were all in the trenches together, working toward goals that seemed worthy, seemed exciting. The computer gaming had to go on hold, and some blowout sleepovers on weekends got canceled. Parents had to give up some of the extended evenings at restaurants or weekend ski trips. Few kids had the usual hours of free time to idly surf the net. But they were engaged, challenged, empowered. It was real. Endorphins were flowing. It was exhilarating.

My father told me about his teenage years in the 1930s. At barely fifteen he was sent to live with a nearby farmer in rural Michigan and served as a hired hand. He slept in an attic room, in which snow sifted through the shingles at night, leaving a frozen dusting on his bed. He ate breakfast at 5:00 a.m. before milking the cows. Then he slogged to school, keeping up straight As. He would return to the farm before supper for the evening chores. It was a regime that few suburban kids today would think they could maintain, but I know they could, and they would feel better about themselves, feel more like real budding men or women because of the chance to contribute. Likewise, year after year, I watch flaccid, failing students make dramatic turnarounds by applying a simple remedy: taking on more work.

For example, take a seventh grade boy who postpones his homework and gives only 15 percent of his attention to anything he writes. Throw him into competitive basketball. Now, his afternoons are swamped, and he gobbles up dinner as if he has not had a meal in days. But in my experience, this kid will begin to turn around his academics too. He is real, he counts, and he believes in hard work for the first time. He has been given the gift of some standing in the world.

Adolescents will find standing and purpose out there however they can. It's what we call cliques, or gangs. It's what we call social media. It's what we sometimes see turn into fanaticism. We have to stop babying them and instead give them more real work, authentic work, hard work. They are desperate for it.

Older people can seldom recall the bursting-out energy of early adolescence. Who can viscerally remember how it was when staying up all night produced only a passing fatigue, when dancing until two in the morning was exhilarating and not tiring, when shivering in the rain on a cold corner for hours with your new boyfriend was pure nirvana? Youth is wasted on the young…if we keep them in the playpen. They are crazy to get out. That energy will explode one way or the other. Harnessing it with authentic work is the only sane solution, for their sake and for the future of our whole society.

20

They Don't Listen; They Watch

The core of our school narrative is instilling grit in our students. In an increasingly crowded and competitive world, grit is essential. We can all recognize grit in action, but it is harder to figure out how people come to be gritty and how this attribute can be cultivated and encouraged.

In her recent book, *Grit: The Power of Passion and Perseverance*, Angela Duckworth explains grit.[16] She describes "gritty" people as hardworking and resilient, with a sense of direction. They become high achievers due to this combination of perseverance and passion. Importantly, she also points to research that shows that children can be inspired to act gritty in the right environments of high expectations and close support.

Adults lead by example in every moment. Adolescents don't listen to us; they watch us. Adults must lead from the front. To partner with and mentor teenagers in work and play that is challenging, authentic, and relevant is both gratifying and appealing to everyone involved. Essential to achieving success with this strategy is to first lay down a foundation of small-group work that promotes relationship and community among teachers and students. This abolishes what I call the "police-state mentality" of many schools: teachers versus students in an endless game of one-upmanship.

Teachers model their own struggles to overcome challenges alongside their students. In addition, teachers decide in partnership with students about how school works, using consensus decision making in Council. Good mentors (which are what the best teachers of adolescents should aim to be) must live the values and behaviors they ask of their students. They must know and respect their students.

Everyone has to follow the rules. Teachers cannot work from atop a hierarchy and convince teenagers to commit to teamwork among their peers. Teachers need to practice what they demand of their students: they must acquire broad knowledge across the whole curriculum, maintain physical fitness, read extensively, turn off media to promote focus, stay informed as global citizens, do the hard physical work.

The model works. It establishes as the culture of the school a community of lifelong learners and collaborators, in which, as Paul Tough says, "Teachers convey to their students deep messages—often implicitly or even subliminally—about belonging, connection, ability, and opportunity."[17] The focus is on "walking the talk" as teachers: modeling positive thinking, taking on challenges, and persevering with hard work.

First and most important, we chant a growth mind-set: "You are learning to be better at this when you work at it every day." It may take hundreds of repetitions, but eventually the lessons will sink in. Adults must model the idea that we simply don't give up; we keep trying.

Second, teachers promise to "show up" for students every day. A parent once explained to me about raising his toddler: "Every morning, as I lift her from her crib, I say, 'Good morning, clean slate,' just to remind myself that I renew my commitment to her every day, and I start over again to try to help her do it a little better."

Third, teachers personally and conscientiously model high expectations, perseverance, and a growth mind-set. We do what many call "leading from the front." If we ask them to learn biology, Spanish, world history, English grammar, and to stay physically fit, we demand the same of ourselves. The science teacher pitches in to teach a few history classes on the Civil War. The English teacher explains quadratic equations in math class when the algebra teacher is called to jury duty. We challenge ourselves. We teach by example.

Duckworth's theory is that skill multiplied by effort leads to achievement. As teachers, we can teach skills, though most likely it will take a lot of repetition. Next, we ask our students to practice the skills relentlessly, and we show up to watch and encourage them. We make a point of demonstrating to them that we, too, are learning new skills and practicing them daily. They watch us struggle as we work hard alongside them.

Three classes in particular provide excellent opportunities for implementing this strategy: PE, public speaking, and Spanish.

PE CLASS

We all know how PE class goes: the kids who are coordinated and energetic can't wait for the class each day, and the kids who are uncoordinated, out of shape, or overweight dread it. In our model, we approach PE by engaging in physical activities that promote fitness and, in practical terms, can be continued throughout a lifetime to maintain a strong body: running, bicycling, jumping rope, walking, hiking, and stretching, as well as recreational tennis and doing calisthenics like jumping jacks or push-ups.

Teachers do the workouts every day alongside the students. This modeling is essential. We let them know that the effort we ask of them, we also ask of ourselves. We commit to maintaining the standards we ask them to meet. When I was injured and could not run laps, I made sure my students noted that I was commuting to school every day on my bike, an equivalent substitution for their running laps.

I have witnessed our strategy working over many years. The stories of a few students in particular are a good illustration. Their stories are in no way unique; they parallel those of several other students that I have taught over the years. Not naturally athletic, these students needed attentive encouragement and tireless leadership from the front to improve their physical fitness. Each kid, like the two profiled here, struggled for months, with some memorable temper tantrums along the way. But in the end, all of them did develop stamina and reached significant physical goals.

—Delia entered our program as a lethargic adolescent who liked to read Harry Potter books again and again, or draw horses. Her parents warned us that she hated exercising and would stubbornly resist participating in PE for the most part. We should expect very little. In the beginning, Delia's behavior mirrored her parents' predictions perfectly. She shuffled instead of running. In tennis, she could take whole minutes to slog across the court to retrieve an errant ball. When we rode bikes, she pedaled so slowly that it was a miracle she could remain upright.

I worked with Delia, as with the other students like her, over the course of two years in PE, cheering myself hoarse. I threw balls back to her from the side of the tennis court. I kept track of her lap times in running and let her know when she shaved off a few seconds or when she relapsed after doing nothing for a whole weekend. I rode beside her on the bike path and kept encouraging and challenging her to pedal a little faster. When she complained she was doing the maximum already, I pointed out that if she were doing her utmost, she would not have enough breath to complain to me that she couldn't do more! I got a kind older student to coach her on how to shift gears properly. Later, Delia saw a loophole and forgot to take her bike home over the weekend to get a flat tire repaired. As a logical consequence, I called her aside during morning break and taught her how to change a flat. She didn't resist, especially since many other students joined her to watch the process in rapt fascination. She rode her bike again with everyone that day in PE.

It took a whole year of this sort of practice and support to begin to break through to Delia. She stolidly maintained her low effort stance class after class, through units of running, playing tennis, biking, and hiking. Nevertheless, she was slowly building up skills, and her performance was subtly improving. More importantly, she never got a "pass" in the class. Never. The rule was solid: if you come to school, you do the work.

At the beginning of Delia's second school year, I could see a glimmer that she was beginning to get it. She reported that she had attended a swimming day camp over the summer, though her ongoing lack of fitness in the first weeks of September made me doubt she had exerted herself very much. In October, we embarked on a rigorous outdoor trip, hiking up a steep waterfall trail in Yosemite and then backpacking deep into the wilderness for a three-day stay. Delia did make it up to the top of the waterfall, albeit very slowly.

She just needed me walking behind her the whole way, chanting, "Left, right, left, right..." as she trudged grimly along. She flashed a mile-wide grin, though, as she celebrated at the top and we snapped a photo of her.

Three days later, we had a five-mile uphill hike to return to our vehicles for the drive home. It was hot, and it was dusty. About two miles into the climb, Delia decided she had reached her limit. Her mood turned evil, and she began kicking up dust, dragging behind the group and cursing her classmates when they urged her to keep up. Eventually, I had to return to the end of the line to hike directly behind her again, alternately cheering and chiding her to keep her pace up.

At the top of a steep incline, Delia fell to pieces. Summoning an impressive amount of energy all at once, she began yelling and threw her pack on the ground. She collapsed into a patch of manzanita shrubs and commenced wailing, slobbering, and screaming obscenities. It was quite a performance. The other kids stood with their mouths open, gawking. This went on for several minutes.

Eventually, I could see Delia was beginning to play out. She was stealing glances out of the corner of her eye to see how we were reacting. I sent the others ahead and then walked over to her in the manzanita patch. "Delia, get up and put your pack on and start walking," I said firmly. She immediately jumped to her feet and screeched right into my face a whole cascade of spit and swear words and tears.

"Well, if you have the energy to do that, I can see you have plenty of energy to keep going. Your performance didn't impress me. I know you can do it, so get up and hit the trail. We will be walking faster from this point on since you still have lots of energy. We have three miles to go. There is no other way out of here, and no one to rescue you. Stop complaining and save your breath."

I didn't know if this would work. But we really did have three miles to go. There truly was no way to be rescued. And she did, in fact, have plenty of energy. The challenge was real. She knew I could not possibly be bluffing. And deep inside, she knew she could do it. She knew I believed she could too.

So she did it.

In fact, we beat our school record for hiking from our campsite to the trailhead. Delia led the group to the finish line. She was silent, yes. She was not walking with what you would call a lilt in her step, but she was doing it. By herself, on her own, she blew through a huge obstacle and got herself to the finish line.

Irrepressibly, her classmates cheered with her as we collapsed at the trail's end. The triumph was obvious, authentic, impressive. It was a turning point for Delia. She started really working in PE class and improved her fitness noticeably over the next months of school.

Delia's story is a common one in a school that firmly maintains a culture of "work hard and you can do it."

—Another student, Lydia, enrolled at age twelve, was still unable to run around the block without falling down. She could not stay upright on a bicycle for more than five minutes without jackknifing and hitting the ground. She could not throw or catch a ball, or jump rope. Over three years, she ran and ran and ran around the block every day. I pedaled beside her on the bike path and suggested when to shift gears, how to position her feet, helped her up when she fell over. We waited for her day after day on group hikes as she trailed far behind. But slowly she improved. She knew there was no "out" for PE, so she just did it. She started to enjoy going fast enough to stay with the group instead of always biking or walking alone. She became interested in seeing her lap times shorten in running. As she departed for high school, she had developed into a good candidate for a sports team, and talked about trying out for crew. Her pride about that was easy to share.

The stories go on and on. Almost every year, we would watch some student abandon his excuses and make a dramatic turnaround in physical effort. For the uncoordinated ones, the overweight ones, the kids who always came in last in elementary school foot races, the discovery of what they could do if they exerted their willpower was the sweetest reward imaginable. What a valuable gift for an adolescent on the cusp of adulthood.

PUBLIC SPEAKING

Public speaking involves a challenge of a different sort, about half-way along the continuum from the physical to the cerebral. The idea of speaking on stage generates enormous fear in most people. Nearly everyone dreads getting up in front of an audience and being judged. Because of this, learning to speak onstage offers an ideal opportunity for instilling perseverance and grit.

Adolescents are emerging from a phase in their lives in which almost every day presents a demand for which they have no previous experience. By the teenage years, all children possess the ability to figure out new skills through trial and error. Public speaking (memorization, body language, presence before an audience, and so forth) is no different, except that adults charge it with a special stigma.

Parents would want to explain to me why their student had to be excused from public speaking. He cannot memorize. He has a lot of social anxiety. She has stage fright. Nevertheless, I have never encountered a teenager incapable of public speaking. In fact, famously, a couple of my students achieved outsize success in tournaments, and they were those whose parents had been the most adamant in their "cannot" statements. Julia came to class supposedly unable to memorize much of anything, from multiplication tables to the Pledge of Allegiance. Damien had such poor working memory that he had trouble repeating a phone number someone had just given him. Dolores crumbled into tears, actually sobbing on the stage, when giving her first speeches. Levon would lose his train of thought and endure an eternal forty seconds of silence on stage, midway through his speech. Jasper had to overcome a tic of twisting his shoulders every other sentence.

Just as in PE class, we set out at the start of the year to build from the ground up. Planning and practice, humility and patience, self-forgiveness and bravado are all part of the lesson plan.

Everyone is lousy at the beginning. The first assignments are fun but instructive. Introduce a fellow classmate to the group. Explain how to make a bed. Invent a use for a broken flashlight or a plastic straw. The group listens to each speaker and laughs, commiserates, and most importantly, applauds. Applause is required after every speech. Attentive listening is mandatory.

As the weeks go by, the speech assignments become more complex. Students give a critical review of a book they read for leisure or a movie they saw last weekend. They try to convince the group on some topical subject: fines for failure to recycle, laws requiring bike helmets, increasing the speed limits on state highways. The group provides a critique after each speech. They will all be giving speeches too and, therefore, quickly come to comprehend the concept of mercy. Every speaker receives written notes from the teacher summarizing audience comments.

Public speaking becomes for students "what we do," not something that is terrifying. If they crash on a first try in class, they can sit down and try again in a few minutes. Some students need to start out by giving speeches in front of just one or two people instead of the whole class. But they understand that no one gets a free pass. Because of this, students simply dig in, and slowly, miraculously, their skills begin to improve. The model is, "All you have to do is give it a try and see how it flies." Criticism is not lethal.

In this way, public speaking becomes another way to practice approaching challenges. Students learn to get up there and do it. Forget the drama. Follow the form. They work their way up to competence under the stage lights.

THE GRIT THEY DEVELOP HELPS WITH OTHER CHALLENGES

As students practice grit in PE and public speaking class, they begin performing better in academic subjects too. A few months after her dramatic tantrum on the trail in the wilderness, Delia stopped ignoring spell-check for her weekly essays and became a more proficient writer. She likewise stopped rebuffing the suggestions to show her step-by-step calculations in math, so she grew there too. After students struggle together running laps or hiking hills, they begin joining the group consensus in problem-solving Councils with more eagerness. The positive mind-set and the understanding that all of us face challenges has a big impact.

I watch a student practice swinging a tennis racket for a few weeks and note improvement. Soon that kid will start to drill daily on math facts, mimicking at home what we do together at the start of every class. He will joke that it's hard, even inhumane torture, but by his eighth grade year, he will have moved into the accelerated math group and be earning excellent grades. Another student improves her physical strength through running, and soon she has better presence on stage delivering speeches. With that under her belt, she starts speaking up in the morning about international news stories she's heard on the way to school. A growing sense of being a competent person infects every corner of a student's life.

SPANISH CLASS AND LEADING FROM THE FRONT TO INSTILL GRIT

Duckworth explains that getting students to act gritty and to work through obstacles is very much dependent on the environment in which they find themselves. They may not be able to maintain the same behaviors and practices once the support is no longer there. This points even more emphatically to the need to create more classrooms in which excellence is demanded and perseverance is expected. This means teachers have to model the behaviors and mind-sets, and they have to lead from the front.

I believed this and had put these ideas into practice for years, focusing on PE and public speaking as the proving grounds. Yet only recently did I understand how broadly effective the model is. It involved teaching Spanish.

When we founded our school in 2005, I planned to teach French as a foreign language because that is my proficiency. In California, however, learning Spanish is critical: over half the population speaks Spanish, and the numbers are climbing. Facing this reality, I spent three months before school opened restudying Spanish. I had been strong in the language when I entered college, but over many years of focusing on French, I was no longer fluent. I set this challenge for myself and worked hard all summer.

I was still a little shaky when school began. So, on the first day of class, I explained to my students that we were all studying Spanish together. "I am further along than you are," I said, "but I am actively working to get better every day. I am drilling at home. You will see me using a dictionary in class. I will need to look up verb conjugations I have forgotten. But I promise I will work hard to meet this challenge, and together we will all improve. We are fellow learners."

This was my cover for teaching something for which I did not feel I was an expert. It turned out to be pure magic to say this to my students. The spirit of the class was electric: all of us were meeting a challenge together. We helped each other, we corrected each other, we offered each other new vocabulary, and we had such fun. Even my dyslexic students lobbied to be "allowed" to take foreign language, a class from which their parents had asked they be excused. We conducted as much conversation as possible in Spanish every day, and soon my coteacher began learning alongside the rest of us too. We had stumbled into a petri dish in which we were the subjects growing our own model. We persevered, we kept a "can do" mind-set, and we worked hard, adults and kids alike.

They don't listen; they watch.

21

How to Stop Sabotaging Education

When we pioneered a new model for middle school education in 2005, we knew we were bucking the trends. But we were convinced that if we were honest with kids, if we walked the talk, and if we provided authentically meaningful experiences, we would be giving our teenage students a gift to last a lifetime. It sounds lofty, but to embark on an adventure outside the envelope, you have to be something of an idealist, or a little bit crazy.

We drew up rules to live by that first year, our tenets. On our first day of class, students read the tenets aloud. There was some rolling of eyes and I noticed lots of facial expressions indicating that everyone had heard all of this before. That evening, students took the tenets home, read them aloud to their parents, and signed the document. Their parents signed the document too.

We kept all of the signed tenets in a file at school. And we pulled them out almost every day for that first month, explaining that, yes, we meant these rules and that we intended to live by them.

This was a shock to everyone, parents included.

REAL School Marin Tenets

- Maintain basic standards of etiquette and kindness. Say please and thank you. Think about the other guy first. Treat others as you would like to be treated. Remember: "The group first, me second."
- Clean up your mess and help others clean up theirs. We all share the space and equipment. Treat it gently and respectfully.
- Come to school rested, prepared, alert, and ready to do your best work.
- There is zero tolerance of substance abuse.
- There is zero tolerance for academic dishonesty or improper computer use.
- Time is precious. Do not waste your time or that of others.
- Think before you speak or act. No "put-downs." Use "I" messages.
- Cleanliness is a virtue. Maintain it in your person and in your surroundings.
- Respect the group and all individuals in it. We are all we have. If we can make it with each other, we can make it anywhere and with anyone on earth.
- Everyone is unique and worthy of respect and attention. When someone "has the floor," the rest of us listen attentively.
- In situations involving issues of safety and appropriateness, teachers have the last word because they have more experience in the world.
- Accepting responsibility for yourself and your own actions is the goal.

- Other guidelines we will figure out as a group as time goes along this year.
- If a student violates any behavior or attitude tenet, the first step will be a conference between the student and teachers. We will write a plan of action for correcting the problem, which will be signed by the student, teachers, and parents. A second violation will result in a parent-student-teacher conference, recorded in writing with a plan of action, including consequences for noncompliance, one of which may be exclusion from overnight trips. Everyone will sign this plan. In the event of a third offense, the student may be asked to withdraw from school.

As the months went by, we as teachers learned how revolutionary it was to these kids to have rules that were solid and consequences that were imposed according to those rules. Holding the line on principles was not quite believable. It was as if, for the first time in their lives, they were being taken seriously, handed responsibility that was meaningful, and expected to carry their own weight. Once they got the idea, they were delirious with their standing. And they were inspired by knowing that this hard work was theirs for real. They came alive.

They had been hungering for this challenge for a long, long time.

We had countless memorable adventures with our students at REAL School Marin. Opening our doors to the kids who came to us, with no formal admissions criteria, we tested our model on all kinds of adolescents. We welcomed students who had been driven from public schools—either for being bratty brainiacs, or for being considered unreachable and unteachable. We taught students who finally thrived after years of feeling bullied in other classrooms, students who pushed through their extreme dyslexia to become writers and speakers, some who overcame paralyzing anxiety or an utter lack of social skills. We taught students who were desperate to be seen, to be known. We also had students who had mastered working the territory by bullying—and we asked them to leave. We enrolled a few students who, despite making significant progress, had parents who could not stand the strain of the endeavor, so they pulled their kids out of the school.

Over a decade of success, we saw that we had crafted a successful formula, one that could reach almost every kid we would encounter. By 2016, I realized I had to put teaching on hold to make time to write about what we had learned in eleven years. There is no such thing as teaching the way a teacher should be doing it, and attempting to give the work less than 100 percent. But our message had to get out: it could be a solution for so much of the dysfunction in today's education system.

Our model is not expensive to operate. It doesn't require lots of hardware, software, fancy technology, smart boards, or any of the other bells and whistles that school reformers seem to consider mandatory for success in education. The discovery we made was basic and born of common sense: the resource we need to offer our teenagers is people who care deeply about holding up standards, who listen, and who believe in their students' potential and push them to their best.

I want to see a hundred more schools like REAL School Marin and thousands more kids turned on to learning and the joy of authentic hard work. I want parents and school reformers to realize they have been pushing for many of the wrong things while overlooking much of the trouble in private schools. Our teenagers cannot wait.

But the darker side of my decision is that I was weary of fighting parents every day for what their kids really needed to grow and mature. I had witnessed so many student triumphs, countless breakthroughs, moments of sheer ecstasy as kids figured out they *could* if only they pulled out all the stops, gritted their teeth, and *sweated*. But still the chorus of parental complaints continued: "You are working him too hard—he cannot do that." Even when kids made undreamed-of progress in dismantling their personal roadblocks, too many parents could not acknowledge the inherent good. Their inability to tolerate watching their kids suffer and struggle blinded them. They could not let go of pushing for better GPAs or guarantees that their kids would get glittering recommendations. We as teachers had to rely on each other for positive feedback and affirmation of what we were accomplishing with students. It was exhausting. Many of the parents just didn't get it.

Yet, every day we teachers celebrated the summits we saw the kids reaching. I see in my mind's eye a dozen teenage boys excitedly reciting poetry by candlelight one night, during a winter outdoor education trip. I remember watching kids give up their lunch hours to finish dissecting a shark. In the desert, they delighted in beating each other to Latin plant identifications, shouting gleefully, "*Opuntia basilaris*" or "*Eriogonum inflatum*," as other kids would the names of rock stars. I recall the games of Curriculum Jeopardy we played every Friday, our students puffed up with pride about their mastery of geography, international events, history, new scientific discoveries. I am so proud of the gap year students who defied peer pressure to spend an extra year consolidating skills so that they could feel more confident and qualified before entering high school. And I remember the boy whose parents claimed he could not organize his belongings or get himself up on time in the morning, so he should bow out of the outdoor education trip. That student took our challenge, practiced diligently for three weeks ahead of the trip, and transformed himself into a model roommate. Someone had assured him he could do it, so he did it. The stories go on and on.

One parent-teacher-student conference made an indelible impact. The student had enrolled in seventh grade, still struggling with elementary math. Her parents met with teachers after school in October, wringing their hands, saying that she was working too hard, she was exhausted. My mind wandered as they whined. Every day at school, she was telling me how excited she was at her progress. At last, someone believed she could do the work, and no one was excusing her from trying. As the parents piled on the complaints, suddenly this courageous young woman interrupted them: "It's ok, Mom and Dad. I am ok with working this hard. I am proud to be accomplishing all of this! I don't need sleep as much as I need this."

But too many parents fought our efforts at every turn. There was a steady drone at the classroom door: "There's too much reading. He cannot memorize scientific terms. It's unfair to give two tests on one day. Her backpack is too heavy. It is outrageous to have to learn the names of world leaders!" I knew these parents loved their kids dearly, but they didn't understand the tricky art of growing up and deep learning, and they were terrified of watching their kids struggle. But their kids, my students, deserved the chance to prove themselves.

Education has gone off track, but it is not too late to set our course right again. In private schools, money's pernicious influence and parents' insistence on customizing the services they purchase sidetrack the conversation about what kids need to grow and how much we can ask of them. Therein lies the big disconnect between parents who lobby on behalf of their kids—but for the wrong things—and teachers who have worked with thousands of teenagers over their careers and know the territory.

It is painful to witness a mighty struggle, but our teenagers need authentic challenges to test themselves. The answer is not to farm our kids out to technology. It's not to dilute face-to-face human connections, which spark real learning. It's not to make everything as push-button easy as possible or to relieve our young people of hard work. Growing up into a solid adult is a difficult, messy, complicated process, and we need to validate that struggle by urging them on with focused attention and strong standards, encouraging them to work harder than they imagine is possible.

We need to stop babying our teenagers and dumbing down their lives. The same loving parents who want to micromanage school to guarantee their kids success could gain so much if they would step aside and trust teachers to stand in for them during those few critical years in which their teenagers are establishing independence, grit, and perseverance.

We need to throw more wilderness and less money at the kids, more "Double down and give it all you have" and less "Let me do it for you, honey." We need to unleash the teenage housekeepers, rescue kids from digital isolation, give them a forum to thrash out moral issues, let them find their own paths outside the race to the highest GPAs.

I know we can improve the education we offer our teenagers. I know we can get there if we give them meaningful work and a sense that their efforts matter. They're dying for us to do it.

Notes

1. Jean M. Twenge, "Insecure: The New Mental Health Crisis," in *iGen: Why Today's Super-Connected Kids Are Growing Up Less Rebellious, More Tolerant, Less Happy—and Completely Unprepared for Adulthood* (New York: Atria Books, 2017), 110–111.
   See also Appendix F, 30–37, http://d1hbl61hovme3a.cloudfront.net/igen-appendix.pdf.

2. "Students Who Contemplated Suicide, 2009–10," CHKS Factsheet #12, G. Austin, S. Cragle, B. Delong-Cotty, and G. Austin, California Healthy Kids Survey, accessed September 1, 2017, chks.wested.org/using-results/factsheets.

3. S. C. Curtin, M. Warner, and H. Hedegaard, "Increase in Suicide in the United States, 1999–2014," NCHS data brief 241(Hyattsville, Maryland: National Center for Health Statistics, 2016), https://www.cdc.gov/nchs/products/databriefs/db241.htm.

4. Amanda Lenhart, "Teens, Social Media & Technology Overview 2015," Amanda Lenhart, Pew Research Center (April 9, 2015), http://www.pewinternet.org/2015/04/09/teens-social-media-technology-2015.

5. Frances E. Jensen and Amy Ellis Nutt, "Building a Brain," in *The Teenage Brain: A Neuroscientist's Survival Guide to Raising Adolescents and Young Adults* (New York: HarperCollins Publishers, 2015), 24–46.

6. Denise Clark Pope, *Doing School* (New Haven: Yale University Press, 2001).

7. Quentin Hardy, "Stay Focused, or Don't," *New York Times*, November 6, 2016.

8. David DeSteno, Cynthia Breazeal and Paul Harris, "The Secret to a Good Robot Teacher," *New York Times, Sunday Review* (August 27, 2017).

9. Angela Duckworth, *Grit: The Power of Passion and Perseverance* (London: Vermilion, 2016), 42.

10. Catherine Steiner-Adair and Teresa H. Barker, "Lost in Connection: How the Tech Effect Puts Children's Development at Risk" in *The Big Disconnect: Protecting Childhood and Family Relationships in the Digital Age* (New York, HarperCollins, 2013), 33-65.

11. Yalda T. Uhls, Minas Michikyan, Jordan Morris, Debra Garcia, Gary W. Small, Eleni Zgourou, and Patricia M. Greenfield, "Five Days at Outdoor Education Camp without Screens Improves Preteen Skills with Nonverbal Emotion Cues," *Computers in Human Behavior* 39 (October 2014): 387–392.

12. Jensen, 83.

13. Amanda Ripley, "Can Teenage Defiance Be Manipulated for Good?" *New York Times*, September 13, 2016.

14. Sebastian Junger, *Tribe: On Homecoming and Belonging* (New York: Twelve, 2016), xvii.

15. John J. Ratey and Eric Hagerman, *Spark: The Revolutionary New Science of Exercise and the Brain* (New York: Little, Brown and Company, 2008), 9–35.

16. Duckworth, 8.

17. Paul Tough, *Helping Children Succeed: What Works and Why* (New York: Houghton Mifflin Harcourt, 2016), 73.

About the Author

Marilyn Englander, PhD, earned her bachelor of arts from Harvard University and her doctorate from the University of California, Santa Barbara. In 2005, she founded the pioneering middle school REAL School Marin. She has over twenty years of experience as an educator and administrator and has led scores of outdoor education adventure trips. Along with her husband, she coauthored *How the Courts Work: A Plain English Explanation of the American Legal System* and is a frequent radio commentator on KQED's *Perspectives*.

Englander has two grown children and lives in the San Francisco Bay Area with her husband.

68022308R00117

Made in the USA
San Bernardino, CA
30 January 2018